"Robert Hotchkin's *Winning* [...]
Emotions delves deep into the [...] ...... encountered by
living Spirit-empowered in all facets of life. This is a breakthrough
book, unlocking profound revelation, practical tools and timely
encouragement for personal revival toward the overcoming victory
gained in Christ alone."

Ché Ahn, president and founder, Harvest International
Ministries; international chancellor, Wagner University

"There are those who are uniquely gifted to shift the atmosphere
from fear to faith. They can skillfully convert the uninformed to
become informed, and ultimately transformed. Robert Hotchkin
is among those anointed wordsmiths that can release a positive
and biblically informed influence on those who read and activate
the powerful revelations and insights in his new book, *Winning the
Battle for Your Mind, Will and Emotions*. Buy it, read it, activate
it in your life."

Dr. Clarice Fluitt, founder and president,
Clarice Fluitt Ministries

"We can have the mind of Christ and walk in wholeness in our
mind, will and emotions. My friend Robert Hotchkin does the
Body of Christ a great favor by writing a compelling book on winning the internal battle. Written in an inspirational and practical
style, this book explains the tools within to help every person walk
in a greater measure of freedom."

James W. Goll, founder, God Encounters Ministries
and GOLL Ideation Music

"The apostle Paul spoke of taking every thought captive to the
obedience of Christ. In other words, we have been granted the
authority from God to control what would otherwise control us.
In *Winning the Battle for Your Mind, Will and Emotions*, Robert
Hotchkin shows from Scripture and personal experience how to
contend in this arena and come out victorious."

Robert Henderson, leader, Global Reformers; bestselling author,
THE COURTS OF HEAVEN series

"Robert does a phenomenal job putting words to what Christians go through on a day-to-day basis. He identifies with readers, then manages to empower them to step into a life of courageous faith. Robert's personal stories are transparent and gripping. It is a must read for all who desire to step into the fullness of what God is calling them to."

Rakesh and Preethy Kurian, senior pastors, Capstone Church

"Robert Hotchkin is a Kingdom leader who genuinely loves people and wants to equip them for victorious Christian living. In his latest book, *Winning the Battle for Your Mind, Will and Emotions*, he lays out solid teaching and strategy to overcome the battles of the mind and live in victory."

Ryan LeStrange, apostolic leader; founder, Ryan LeStrange Ministries; author, *Hell's Toxic Trio*

"Personally, I don't know anyone—including myself—who has mastered their thought life. I'm so glad Robert Hotchkin has given us a valuable resource to help us keep our thinking in line with God's thinking, which is the key to success and happiness in life."

Roberts Liardon, pastor, Roberts Liardon Ministries and Embassy International Church

"Wow—to be able to live and function in the fullness of Christ's presence, power and personality! This is *far more* than just another how-to manual on victorious living! Robert offers Spirit-led insights on our ability to recognize and choose truth over responding to the enemy's lies in the midst of life's intense, challenging and often fearful circumstances. In reading this book, you will become enlightened, equipped and empowered to win your own personal inner battles."

Mary Audrey Raycroft, founder, Releasers of Life; teaching pastor, Catch the Fire, Toronto, Ontario

"The wisdom of God drips off the pages of this book. Chapter after chapter will impart to you solutions to many of your life battles. Secrets for success are unlocked, wisdom for your personal struggles is imparted and strength to make wise decisions is waiting to be given to you! *Winning the Battle for Your Mind, Will and Emotions* will set you free to be the overcomer you are meant to be. Read this book to be a champion. Share this book with someone to be a blessing. Live the contents of this book to become a gate of heaven on earth!"

Brian Simmons, translator, The Passion Translation Project

"Robert Hotchkin's ability to practically communicate biblical precepts is superb. In *Winning the Battle for Your Mind, Will and Emotions*, he takes my favorite subject—the soul—and gives us a feast of fresh revelation that has a breaker anointing on it. I consider myself well versed on the subject of inner healing, yet Robert has one-upped me with this anointed book. You are going to love it, but even more, you are going to be freed and healed in *every* area of your life as you read it and apply its truth."

Katie Souza, founder, Katie Souza Ministries
and Expected End Ministries

"This is one of the most helpful, practical and biblical books on the transformation of the mind, will and emotions that you will read this year. This is the battle manual we have been waiting for. Get ready for victory."

Darren Stott, lead pastor, Seattle Revival Center

"Robert Hotchkin has written a great book on overcoming in our mind, will and emotions. It is so practical, so personal and so biblical. I know Robert; he is an extremely honoring person. In this book he honors God and His ability to help us break through every soul issue. This book is so Robert! Most of all it is so true of his own character. This is written by a man who lives this. The book is excellent, and I highly recommend Robert Hotchkin!"

Barbara J. Yoder, lead apostle, Shekinah Regional Apostolic
Center and Breakthrough Apostolic Ministries Network

WINNING
the
BATTLE
FOR YOUR MIND, WILL *and* EMOTIONS

ROBERT HOTCHKIN

Chosen

a division of Baker Publishing Group
Minneapolis, Minnesota

Published by Chosen Books
11400 Hampshire Avenue South
Bloomington, Minnesota 55438
www.chosenbooks.com

Chosen Books is a division of
Baker Publishing Group, Grand Rapids, Michigan

Printed in the United States of America

ISBN 978-0-8007-9887-1

Library of Congress Cataloging-in-Publication Control Number: 2018019480

Cover design by Rob Williams, InsideOutCreativeArts

18 19 20 21 22 23 24   7 6 5 4 3 2 1

Dedicated to:

The King of Glory, the Lord Almighty, the Lord Invincible who has won every battle—including the battle for our mind, will and emotions—so that we can live in the fullness of victory and operate in the fullness of His presence, power and personality all the days of our lives.

And to every believer who has persevered in faith, choosing to believe the eternal truth of God's Word over the report of his or her temporary circumstances. I honor you as the champion of faith, dominion steward and agent of impact that you are.

Contents

Foreword

In a world filled with spiritual confusion, moral decline and intentional corruption, we desperately need to know how to win the battle for the mind, will and emotions! The devil is a liar. In fact, Jesus called him the father of lies and disclosed that he "does not stand in the truth because there is no truth in him. Whenever he speaks a lie, he speaks from his own nature" (John 8:44).

Oh yes, the devil is a big liar! He cannot speak the truth. Most of the time, the exact opposite of anything he would speak into your thoughts is true. For example, he may attempt to fill your mind with thoughts like these: *You're a loser. You're a failure. You're rejected by God and man. You're sick and dying. You're destined for lack and poverty.* The exact opposite is true! The Word has the final and eternal say on the matter, and it declares that you are an overcomer, a champion, an object of God's love and affection, favored by God and man, alive, well, full of strength and vitality and living in divine abundance. How do I know this is true? Because the Word reveals the truth.

11

Jesus *is* truth. Truth is His nature, and the word He speaks is truth, spirit and life (see John 6:63; 10:10; 17:17).

Here is the issue plain and simple: If you believe a lie, you will manifest the fruit of that lie, but if you believe the truth, you will manifest the fruit of that truth. It seems so simple, and it is: Believe the devil's lies and you will experience death, loss and destruction, but if you believe the truth of Jesus, you will experience life in its abundance. It is such a simple decision, yet so many people struggle internally and end up making decisions in favor of the devil's lie. Why? It is usually because we do not understand how to discern the battlefield.

This battle needs to be fought and won, but you will not find this battle on land, sea or air. This battle is in your mind, will and emotions—your soul. Every battle you face can be won every time, and the more you practice winning, the more you win.

I remember that as a young woman, I was defeated constantly in certain areas of life due to giving in to lies. I did not know they were lies, and neither did I understand the reality of the devil or that he was behind them. I simply concluded that the lies were my own thoughts, beliefs and feelings. They all seemed so legitimate, making total sense according to the circumstances I was in. As a result, I believed that I was rejected, oppressed, depressed, weak and broken, because it all seemed so real. Something can appear real, yet be so far from the truth.

I needed *truth* as a plumb line not only to expose the lie, but also to use the truth as a powerful weapon in the battle for the mind, will and emotions. Everything in life flows from the soul. Scripture alerts us to watch over our heart with all diligence, because from it flow the issues of life (see Proverbs 4:23).

If all the issues of life flow from your soul (mind, will and emotions), then it makes sense that this part of you is what the enemy will choose to target. If he can control your thoughts, feelings and decisions, he can control your life.

I slowly, over time, learned to fight this war for the soul with the weapon of truth, and as I persevered in the battle, I experienced more and more victories. Robert Hotchkin's invitation to encounter victory in the battle for the soul is for every believer to embrace.

Robert is a man I have known for many years. I have witnessed him battle through intense warfare in his soul, and I have watched him prevail over and over again. He learned to turn what appeared to be stumbling blocks into stepping-stones that brought him to a place of greater glory and testimony. He can help you do the same as he discloses valuable nuggets of "manna" from heaven that he learned from the presence of God in the midst of battle.

Robert does not write merely from a place of understanding spiritual principles on this subject, but rather from a place of experience in warring with the truth and for the truth. As a result, he is well qualified as a seasoned veteran to give you valuable input on this subject and to impart fortifying revelation that will greatly empower and establish you.

You were created to win, to be the head and not the tail, above and not beneath. It is time to arise and shine. Your light has come. Stand in this truth, which is your strength, for *you* are a champion in Christ!

Patricia King, founder, Patricia King Ministries

Acknowledgments

My name may be on the cover of *Winning the Battle for Your Mind, Will and Emotions*, but by no means was this a solo effort. There are many people who, in many ways, have helped make this book all that it is. There have also been several key people in my life who have helped make me the writer, and the man, that I am. They all deserve acknowledgment and my heartfelt thanks.

Jane Campbell, editorial director of Chosen Books. This book would not exist without the wise, witty and wonderful Jane Campbell. It all began from a conversation we had during a group dinner at one of our large conference events. Many others were there who were more well-known and more important, and yet, Jane, you were never in a hurry to move on from the flow of revelation I rambled through. At the end of that dinner, you encouraged me to share any ideas I might have for a project we could work on together. And here we are. Thank you, my friend.

Trish Konieczny, editor supreme! Okay, that is not Trish's official title at Chosen, but it sure is an accurate description. Thank you so much, Trish, for all your help. Those query boxes of yours were filled with wisdom and overflowing with heart. Just like you.

The whole team at Chosen Books and Baker Publishing Group: Shaun, Natasha, Carra, Chris, Anna, Patnacia and so many more. Thank you all for all you have done to help make *WTB* all that it is.

My wonderful wife. Thank you, Yu-Ree, for your love and support during the many, many hours I spent at the computer instead of with you and our family while I was working on *WTB*. You are not only a very clever squirrel; you are also a very understanding one!

My sister, Carol, who has always been my friend and champion. And who is also one of the greatest examples I know of someone who has grabbed hold of Jesus and won the battle for her mind, will and emotions. Thank you for being the best big sister ever.

My mother, Ellen. Thanks, Mom, for instilling in me a great love of language, books and writing. And for all those trips to the library every week during summer vacations!

Bart Hadaway. For years you were my pastor. You will always be my friend. Thank you for being there for me in some of my biggest battles. I could not have asked for a better confidant or more loyal ally.

Our Patricia King Ministries family. Every single one of you was so encouraging, supportive and understanding during the process of creating this book. It is a privilege to serve with you all. Thank you for loving Jesus so passionately, and for the privilege of being on your team!

Ron and Patricia King. Anything I ever do for the Kingdom is unto your accounts in heaven, my dear friends. You took a brand-new Christian under your wings and loved me, mentored me, encouraged me, poured into me and stood by me. Over and over again. "Thank you" does not cover it, but you sure deserve to hear it.

And most of all, I want to acknowledge the Holy Spirit. My God, my Teacher, my Comforter, my Wisdom, my Helper and my Friend. Thank You for filling me, surrounding me, overflowing me and being with me every step of the way on this book and in my life. I honor You, adore You and appreciate You more than words can communicate.

Introduction

The Eternal Truth of I AM

For they exchanged the truth of God for a lie.

Romans 1:25

Heaven is only a decision away.

This is one of the most important truths that any Christian will ever realize. The reason it is so key to know—to grab hold of, to live inside of, to believe as a deep and immovable truth—is because it seems at times that heaven and the fullness of God's Kingdom are not available to us. The enemy and his minions work overtime to lie and lure us into believing the report of our temporary circumstances, as opposed to the eternal truth that God is good, He loves us very much and He has made available to us all we need through the gift of His Son and the finished work of the cross. His Kingdom is ours, all the time, no matter what. All we have to do is to agree. Simple. Not always easy, but simple.

God is present tense. He is the Great I AM (Exodus 3:14). Not the Great I Was, or the Great I Will Be. He and His Kingdom are always present and always great, always there and always victorious (see Joshua 1:5, 9; Psalm 24:8). That means anything we have ever had or experienced of Him or with Him is still ours. It also means that there is nothing we are looking forward to from Him or in Him that is not ours already—not just one day in the sweet by-and-by, but right now, in Christ. When we as Christians get this—really grab hold of it as *truth* so that we never surrender this triumph in Christ—it will change how we think, how we pray, how we respond, how we live and how we contend for greater manifestations of what we know is already ours. When we understand who He is and what He has accomplished, we will shift from waiting for God to do something to knowing that He already has. We will go from crying out for change to realizing we have been empowered by the finished work of our victorious Risen Lord to be His change agents in the earth. We will no longer be overwhelmed by our feelings, but instead, we will be triumphant in our faith. We will be transformed from pitiful to powerful, from worriers to warriors, from ordinary to extraordinary, from natural to supernatural.

This is the battle—your battle. When grief from your past, the challenges of your present or fear for your future try to tell you that God is not there or that He does not care, the eternal truth of "I AM" can arise in you and trump everything—past, present, future, fear, feelings, frustration, all of it. If, in those moments, you will choose to believe Him above all else, you will be victorious.

Yes, this is the battle, but even more important than recognizing the battle is realizing where it takes place. It is in your soul—your mind, will and emotions. Your soul is where you feel and think and believe and decide. It is the place of volition. It is where you exercise the profoundly powerful gift of your free will.

The battle is real, and at times it is intense. But we are not in the battle alone. We have a champion. His name is Jesus, the Great I AM (see John 8:58; Revelation 1:8). And the truth is that He has already won this battle for us (see John 19:30; 1 John 3:8). His Holy Spirit works constantly to remind us of this, so we may choose to live inside Christ's victory all the days of our lives, and in every situation we encounter (see John 14:26; 2 Corinthians 2:14).

The battle has always been in the soul. Not just for you and me, but for everyone who has ever walked with the Lord. Look at Moses. He had to win this battle of the soul and make the choice of whether or not to believe his past and current circumstances, or to trust in what the Great I AM had for him. For many years, Moses had been tending someone else's sheep on the back side of nowhere (see Exodus 2–3). The report of his past was that he was an unwanted failure. When he had stepped out to be a deliverer of his people, the Israelites, it had not gone well. They had rejected him, and he had been forced to flee for his life (see Exodus 2:11–15). Then year after year, out wandering around the wilderness, he must have felt as though he was getting further and further from the promise over his life, and even from God Himself. His current circumstances declared that his best years were behind him and he was, more than likely, an also-ran who would never do anything of any real impact or merit. This is when God showed up and declared Himself "I AM," reminding Moses that the gifts, callings and promises of the Great I AM do not expire, because He is always present and always present tense.

God let Moses know that He had seen and heard all that he and Israel had been through, and that Moses was the deliverer of the Israelite people. Nothing had changed. No past failures or current difficulties were greater than the truth, reality and power of who God was, what He had planned and His ability to bring it forth in the now—no matter what. But Moses had to choose to believe this. He had questions about himself, and questions about Israel. The Lord's answer to all of it was "I AM." In other words, despite how things must have looked or felt, and regardless of how long they had looked or felt that way, Moses' destiny was as present tense as ever because I AM was as present tense as ever.

The enemy works overtime to remind us of our failures and disappointments, hoping to convince us that nothing will ever work out the way we want. He pokes at us with present challenges so that we will choose to believe that things will always be challenging. The enemy wants us to feel defeated so that we give up, give in and quit believing. Getting us to do that is the only victory he has available to him. He is defeated, so he wants us to feel that way, too.

The enemy's strategy in the battle for the mind, will and emotions is to get us to confuse the temporary "now" with the eternal I AM. He works constantly to trick us into believing the lie that past failures and present difficulties are our portion. No. God—all that He is, all He has done and all He has given us—is our portion. We have been fully restored to relationship with the Great I AM. We are grafted into the present-tense certainty of the fullness of His victory and Kingdom.

The enemy is defeated. He knows it, just as he knows that his only real opportunity is to try to manipulate the gift of our free will—to make us believe the lie that we, not he, are cast down. The way he does this is to highlight temporary circumstances and challenges, poking at our feelings and stirring up fear, frustration, doubt, offense and self-pity so that we will choose to exchange the eternal truth of I AM for a lie of Satan. The enemy wants us to come into agreement with how things look and feel right now. He wants to get us mired in murmuring, complaining and cursing. But we can win the battle for our mind, will and emotions by choosing to trust in the always-truth of I AM and coming into agreement with His Word, His victory and His no-matter-what faithfulness. Then instead of murmuring, complaining and cursing, we will find ourselves praising, worshiping, interceding and decreeing. And in that, we will know victory, and we will break through into greater manifestations of what has been ours all along—His fullness!

I learned the power of this type of soul shift firsthand years ago, while in the midst of a decade-plus battle to overcome serious and mysterious health challenges. At one of my lowest points—after working with numerous doctors in multiple cities and countries, spending all kinds of money and enduring just about every test and procedure—I was feeling sicker and weaker than ever. In that moment I was frustrated, discouraged and afraid. One morning I cried out to God, complaining about how unfair my sorry state was. I told Him that I had prayed every prayer I could think of, decreed the Word again and again, stood in faith and had nothing left. There was nothing else I could think of to do.

Very quietly He spoke to my heart, saying, *I want you to thank Me for the health and strength you have right now.*

My immediate response was to shoot back out loud, "What health? What strength?" I was angry, even offended. I wanted to shout back how unfair it was that I was barely able to get out of bed and make it to my prayer chair. I was caught up in self-pity. And I was misunderstanding what He was leading me to do. I was making the mistake of thinking that praising Him for what I had was the same thing as accepting my current set of circumstances. I was allowing how things looked and felt in the "now" to mire me in the muck of fear, frustration, self-pity and offense. I was feeling sorry for myself, and in that, choosing to be pitiful instead of powerful. In other words, I was losing the battle for my mind, will and emotions.

But the Lord! Again He nudged me to praise Him for the strength I had. Almost begrudgingly, I decided to do it: "Fine. Praise You, Lord, for the strength I have in my body right now."

Much to my surprise I felt a faint stirring, the beginning of a shift. Not in my body so much as in my soul. I said it again: "Praise You, Lord, for the strength I have in my body right now." As soon as I did, more bubbled up: "Thank You, Lord, that I had the strength to get out of bed. Thank You that I had the strength to walk to my prayer chair. And thank You that I have breath in my lungs and strength in my body to praise You and give You thanks this morning." And I meant it.

The more I chose to give thanks and the more I chose to praise Him—the more I chose to take command of my soul and bring it into alignment with the truth that radiated from my born-again spirit—the more I chose to do this, the easier and easier it was to lift myself out of the muck and mire of the temporary "now" and rejoice in the truth of the eternal I AM. A knowing arose in me. A certainty came back into my soul. I would not be offended and downcast by my current circumstances. Instead, I would declare that the offense was the illegal attack of sickness against my body, and I would cast down those symptoms again and again in faith and certainty, until I saw the full manifestation of the truth of I AM, in whom I was strong, healed and filled with the fullness of life (see John 10:10). That was my portion! That was my truth! I chose to believe it. I chose to rejoice in it. And I chose to praise Him for it. All through the power of my will.

The will is how we take command of the soul. We choose to do it. If it seems odd that we use a part of our soul—the will—to keep our soul under control, think of it like this: You use a part of your car—the steering wheel—to keep your car under control. When you get in and buckle up, you choose to take control of your car via the steering wheel. You don't have to do it that way. You could just as well punch the gas and see what happens. But that would not be wise. In wisdom, you put your hands on the steering wheel so that you can take control of where your car goes. It is the same thing with your will and your soul. Think of the steering wheel as your will, and the car as your soul. We choose in our soul, via our will, to take command of our soul and to steer it. By choosing to praise and give thanks instead of complaining or murmuring, I was taking control of my soul. I was steering it. Instead of allowing the "car" of my soul to go careening wildly about from feeling to feeling or thought to thought, I used my will to steer my soul into giving thanks and praise.

This was not just a onetime thing. Taking control of my soul was a weapon I discovered I could wield again and again. Almost every morning, I would begin my day by choosing to praise God at least ten times in a row. Some days I even counted them off: "Praise the Lord, O my soul, and all that is within me . . . one! Praise the Lord, O my soul, and all that is within me . . . two! Praise the Lord, O my soul, and all that is within me . . . three!" And so on. The more I took command of my soul and caused it to come into agreement with the eternal truth of the Spirit of I AM within me, the more I could feel increase—not only of faith, but also of power and authority. I would be stirred not only to take command of my soul, but also of my body: "Praise the Lord, O my soul, and all that is *within* me. Praise the Lord, my *liver*! Praise the Lord, my *heart*! Praise the Lord, my *lungs*! Praise the Lord, my *thyroid*! Praise the Lord, my *blood*! Praise the Lord, my *immune system*!"

I would name every system, every organ and every gland in my body that was struggling or failing, and I would command it to praise the Lord. By faith, I could feel the shift moving from my soul into my body. I knew that all of heaven and the fullness of life, health and strength were mine *right now* because of His love for me and because of the amazing gift of the finished work of the cross. And I would praise the Great I AM yet again.

The morning in my prayer chair that I began with feeling sorry for myself ended with discovering the power of taking command of my soul. It was a marker in time for me, much like the burning bush encounter with the Great I AM was for Moses. That morning was when the Lord began to teach me how to win the battle for my mind, will and emotions. I can look back and see that from that day forward, there was an increase of breakthroughs and improvements. It was not always steady. It was not always fast. But there had been a shift for sure in my soul. And in time, also a shift in my body, to the point where I now enjoy a noticeable and dramatic improvement in my health and strength. I am able, once again, to travel the world and preach. And I operate in a greater level of authority in those meetings, I believe, because of the greater levels of authority the Lord taught me to operate in over my *self*. When we co-labor with God to take the inner territory of our mind, will and emotions, there is no outer territory that will be able to stand against His truth and our faith in it (see Joshua 1:3–5; Mark 11:22–24).

I believe the reason you have this book in your hands right now is because you have come to your marker in time—just like that morning in my prayer chair for me and that day at the burning bush for Moses. As you read these pages, you will be enlightened, equipped and empowered. You will not only come to see the battle for what it is; you will also discover how to walk in victory. The enemy will no longer be able to steal from you. Feelings and fears will no longer control you. You will go from being overwhelmed by circumstances to being an overcomer who knows truth and operates in faith. All of heaven is yours, right now. *Winning the Battle for Your Mind, Will and Emotions* will help you see and agree with that reality, so that you can tear down every lie of the enemy and live in the fullness of blessing that is yours in Christ.

1

In the Beginning

Then God said, "Let us make man in our image, after our likeness. And let them have dominion."

Genesis 1:26 ESV

From the very beginning, we can clearly see the heart and plan of the Father—to have a people in the earth who are fully His and fully operating in His authority, on His behalf. We were created from relationship, for relationship, and in that relationship we are to be His expression into all of creation. Because of who made us, and because of how we are made, we are able to inhabit the earth as His dominion stewards—His agents of impact—expressing the reality of Him and His Kingdom throughout all of creation, all the time, wherever we are and in whatever situations we find ourselves.

At the very beginning of the Bible, God reveals who He is, what He does and how He does it. The first three verses of Genesis 1 say this:

In the beginning God created the heavens and the earth. The earth was formless and void, and darkness was over the surface of the deep, and the Spirit of God was moving over the surface of the waters. Then God said, "Let there be light"; and there was light.

In this amazing opening salvo of revelation, God puts on display that He is the Creator. He shows us that He is well able to create something from nothing, and that He also brings order and light to chaos and darkness, immediately and easily.

Looking a bit further into the passage, not only do we see who God is and what He does, but we also get key insights into how He does it, starting with the very first mention of "God" in verse 1. The Hebrew word used for God here is *Elohiym*. It carries the meaning "supreme God" or "God above all gods." What is so interesting (and revealing) about this word is that it is plural. The very first mention of God in the Bible shows that He is a plurality, a relationship. Our God is One, but He shows us at the very beginning of the Bible that He is One made up of three distinct Persons. He then goes on throughout Scripture to reveal these Persons as Father, Son (the Word) and Holy Spirit. I realize that the topic of the Godhead is huge, and I am not trying to open a massive theological can of worms here, but it is important for us to see that our God, in whose image we are made, is One, and in that One is a Three-in-One relationship in perfect order, union, harmony and communion. In seeing this, we then begin to get insight into how it is God does what He does.

In verses 2 and 3 of Genesis 1, the power and impact of this united plurality co-laboring as One is made evident. We see in verse 2 that the earth was formless and void, and that there was darkness everywhere. But the Spirit of God begins to hover and move. Then in verse 3 God sends forth the Word. As God the Father, the Spirit and the Word (the Son) all worked together as a perfectly united relationship within the One, light broke forth and divine order was established. This is how the world was brought forth.

Our God is Three-in-One—Father, Son (Word) and Spirit—always in perfect relationship, harmony, order and unity. This is how the Creator creates—as a unified cooperation of agreement. This constant and continual divinely ordered harmony, in a united expression of the will and ways of the One, is what brings forth His plans and purposes from the unseen realm into the seen realm. This is how the supernatural becomes quite literally natural. This is why, at a word, darkness is totally and utterly shattered. This is how chaos is quickly and easily turned into divine order.

This agreement of the Three-in-One may strike you as a "duh." After all, of course the Father, Son and Holy Spirit are all in agreement. They are One. But the reason this is so important for you to see is because you are made in His image and made to be His expression in the earth. An important key to being effective in this mandate is to see and understand the way He does it—as a harmonious co-laboring of the Three-in-One. In that harmony, He displays for us, the ones made in His image, how we can be successful in carrying out what we are called to do in His dominion authority in the earth, on behalf of Him and His Kingdom.

Made in His Image

After bringing forth all of creation (see Genesis 1:1–25), God crowned His works by creating man and giving us dominion authority over all the earth and everything in it:

> Then God said, "*Let Us make man in Our image, according to Our likeness; and let them rule* over the fish of the sea and over the birds of the sky and over the cattle and over all the earth, and over every creeping thing that creeps on the earth." *God created man in His own image, in the image of God He created him; male and female He created them.* God blessed them; and God said to them, "Be fruitful and multiply, and *fill the earth, and subdue it; and rule.*"
>
> Genesis 1:26–28 (emphasis added)

We see from these verses that the "Us" of God—Father, Son and Spirit—created us male and female in Their image, to be Their representation in the earth. That our Three-in-One God made us in His image is key. Just as God is Three-in-One, so also are you three-in-one. He made you body, soul and spirit and declared the totality of you (in proper relationship with Him) as "very good" (Genesis 1:31). I am not saying, of course, that our three "parts" are the same as the Three-in-One Persons of the Trinity. Rather, I am saying that our "parts" need to operate in harmony, too—a unified harmony of right relationship with God. This is the key to operating effectively in dominion authority as His representative in the earth. To be "in His image." To be three-in-one, as He designed and intended—a right relationship of body and soul with born-again spirit—all working together according to His will, ways, character and nature.

God begins the Bible in Genesis 1 by showing us His Three-in-One self cooperating in divine unity to shatter darkness, establish divine order and bring forth creation. He then creates us to be His creative expression. This is not just a history lesson. In those initial 25 verses of the Bible's first chapter, God is not only bringing forth all of creation; He is also modeling to us, as His made-in-His-image dominion stewards of that creation, how to do the job He appoints us to in verses 26–28. We are three-in-one, made in the image of the Three-in-One and made to operate in a similar unified harmony of cooperation. When our three "parts"—body, soul and spirit—are in right relationship with God (under His authority) and in right relationship with each other, then we are true "re-presentations" of Him in the earth. And it is very good!

What is not very good is when our body, soul and spirit are not cooperating in unity and agreement with God's will, ways, character and nature. We best represent and reflect God's image when we are a unified three-in-one, not when we are three parts going their own ways. An obvious example of this disunity would be a Christian whose born-again spirit is connected deep-unto-deep with God, but his body is engaging in sexual sin and his soul is filled with anger and negativity. That Christian is still, of course, three-in-one in the sense that he is one person with a body, soul and spirit. But he is not operating as a true, harmonious three-in-one reflection of the Three-in-One God in whose image he is made. The born-again spirit of that errant Christian is connected with God, but his body and his soul are not in right relationship with God, nor are they in right relationship with each other. The actions of his body and the thoughts, emotions and choices of his soul are not in harmony with the truth of God that is known and always adhered to by his born-again spirit. This errant Christian, though still one person with three parts, is not a harmonious three-in-one agreement expressing the fullness of God into the earth. This is not the place of true victory and power. This is not how God originally created us to be, and it is not what we as born-again Christians are re-created for through Jesus.

Free to Choose

We are made in God's image. We are divinely designed to be three-in-one—a flowing harmony of our body, soul and spirit united in relationship and agreement with Him. From that relationship, we then express Him into the earth in powerful ways that shatter darkness and bring divine order in the midst of confusion and chaos. This is who we truly are. This is what we truly are made for. What determines whether or not we fully walk in this place of harmony, victory, authority, influence and divine power? Our soul.

Our soul is the "place" of our mind, will and emotions. It is where we think our thoughts, feel our feelings and make our choices. It is the seat of the great gift of free will that the Lord has blessed us with, where we are free to choose whether we will trust in God and follow Him and His ways as the new creations we are in Christ, or follow the desires of our old carnal nature and come out of agreement with God. It is all about the choices we make. And just to be clear, I am not talking about choosing to enter into a works-based religion that would try to convince us that pious performance or self-righteousness gives us favor with God and thus earns us an ability to move in His authority. I am talking about embracing and valuing above all else the relationship we have through Christ, which plugs us into all that God is and all that we were originally created for. And then within that relationship, *choosing* to agree with who we truly are in God by *choosing* to trust in His goodness, and believing in Him and His eternal truth over any report of temporary circumstances, fearful thoughts or runaway feelings.

When we receive Jesus Christ as our Lord and Savior, we are born again and His Holy Spirit gives us "new life." The *Father* does for each of us who receive the gift of His *Son* through His *Holy Spirit* what He did for all of creation in Genesis 1:2–5. Our Three-in-One God overcomes our darkness with His light, establishes His Kingdom order in the midst of what was our chaos and brings forth glorious new life (see 2 Corinthians 5:17). We fully receive this new life into our born-again spirit, which is made brand-new and complete in Christ (see John 1:1–13; 3:3–6). Our born-again spirit is perfect. It does not sin. It does not rebel. It is always in harmony with God and His Kingdom, submitted to the leading of His Holy Spirit (see Romans 8:9–10; 1 John 3:9). When our body and soul are aligned with our born-again spirit, we are agreeing with and flowing in the truth and reality that we are made in God's image—a three-in-one reflection and representation of the Three-in-One. We choose whether or not to be in agreement with this truth. We choose whether or not to bring our body and soul into alignment with our perfect born-again spirit through the actions we choose to take, the thoughts we choose to focus on and the feelings we choose to be filled with. We make all of these choices in our soul.

In Deuteronomy 30:19 God says, "I have set before you life and death, the blessing and the curse. So *choose* life in order that you may live" (emphasis added). We often think of this in terms of our salvation, and certainly when we choose Jesus as Lord and Savior, we choose life. But this is not only about coming to know Christ. We have the choice of life and death, blessing and curse, before us in every decision we make. Will we choose to trust in and follow the will and ways of our good God so that we continue to inhabit the fullness of life, blessing, victory and empowerment? Or will we choose to give in to the lusts of the flesh and the lures and lies of the enemy, which appeal to our old selfish, prideful,

I-me-mine fallen nature? We make that decision in our soul. In any given moment, and in every situation we face, it is our soul that chooses whether we will trust, believe and abide in God. The arena for the battle of life versus death and blessing versus curse is our soul. This is why the soul realm, the realm of our mind, will and emotions, is the main target of the enemy, and it has been since the beginning.

A Snake in the Garden

The enemy often understands the impact and importance of our mind, will and emotions better than we do. From the very beginning, Satan has grasped the power that those of us in relationship with God have through the decisions we make: power for life or death, blessing or curse, for us and for all of creation. We see this clearly in Genesis 3:1–7, when Satan comes to Eve in the Garden. Depending on the translation you use, Scripture points out that this snake of an enemy is more shrewd, crafty, clever or cunning than any other creature (see Genesis 3:1). The Hebrew word for it is *aruwm*, from the root *aram*. In all of its various English translations, the word implies an ability and desire to manipulate. This is exactly what the enemy does to Eve, first by questioning God's word so that she gets up in her head about what God "really" said, and then by appealing to her pride and appetites to make disobeying God seem like an appealing choice (see Genesis 3:1, 5). When we read this passage, we see the deceitfulness of the enemy and how he lures Eve in, but it is important to grasp that she made the decision. She had the power to obey or disobey, to believe and trust in God's goodness and wisdom or not. It was her choice, a choice she made in her soul. Look at Genesis 3:6:

The woman was *convinced.* She saw that the tree was beau-
tiful and *its fruit looked delicious,* and *she wanted the wisdom it would give her. So she took* some of the fruit and
ate it.

Genesis 3:6 NLT, emphasis added

The temptation to disobey appealed to her appetites (the
fruit looked delicious) and to her pride (she wanted forbidden wisdom), but the decision whether or not to let those
temptations be more appealing than the truth of God's word
and the reality of His character and nature was made in her
soul. The battle is ultimately always in the soul realm—the
place of decision and volition.

Adam had the same decision to make. It was his choice
whether he would value dwelling in the fullness of relationship, provision, protection, fellowship and communion with
God in the Garden by trusting in the truth and wisdom of
His word, or choose to deny and disobey the Lord's clear
instructions. Just like Eve, he chose to disobey. The result
was a curse coming upon them and all of creation. As we
saw earlier, we are God's dominion stewards in the earth.
The decisions we make not only affect us; they affect all of
creation.

Nothing Is Missing

Adam and Eve made a bad decision in the Garden. That is
clear. But what may not be as immediately evident is *why*
they made that bad decision. What was the temptation of
the enemy that was powerful enough to get them to value a
bite of that one forbidden fruit above all else God had given
them and blessed them with? We see it in Genesis 3:5: "Your

eyes will be opened when you eat it. *You will become just like God*" (NLT, emphasis added).

The temptation was to be "like" God. The irony of this is that they already were made in His image! Genesis 1:26–27 makes it clear that Adam and Eve, just like you and me, were made in the very image of God. In relationship with Him, they enjoyed all the fullness of who He is and all He had given them. There was not one thing they lacked. The Garden was where heaven overlapped earth. In that place there was total provision, perfection and protection. It was the place of union and communion with God and His Kingdom. The lie behind the enemy's temptation was that there was something "missing"—that something else, something external was needed to be fully who and what God created them to be. The lie was that God was keeping "something" from them. No!

God made us in His very likeness. He has given us everything. His Word and instructions are not to control, limit or keep things from us. Just the opposite! They are to keep us from harm so that we can fully enjoy the fullness of who He is, how He made us and all that we are created for and blessed with. That is what He wanted for Adam and Eve, and what He wants for all of us today—to know that in Him, we have been given everything. In the greatness of I AM, we have all the fullness of who He is, all He has done and all He has given us. Right now. Nothing is missing. Nothing else is needed. If it ever looks or feels that way, it is a temporary lie that we must stand against by choosing to stand on the eternal truth of I AM.

Adam and Eve were made in the image of the Creator. They were divinely designed to be His creative expression, stewarding all of creation. But because they did not first and foremost steward the realm of their soul, instead of helping create godly order in the earth—filling it with limitless light and life—they created separation, division, fear, shame and pain (see Genesis 3:11–24). Because they did not watch over and steward the interior realm of their mind, will and emotions and choose to operate as a three-in-one representation of God in whose image they were made, the exterior realm they were entrusted with was cursed instead of blessed. Our decisions matter; they have impact.

Same Old Enemy, Same Old Tactics

From the beginning, we were created to steward creation on behalf of God, in the place He created for us. Literally in the place He made for us to dwell with Him, where heaven overlapped earth (Eden), and figuratively in the place of being His representatives to all of creation. When Adam and Eve rebelled against God, they were banished from the place of God, where heaven overlapped earth. They were cast out of Eden and were no longer His dominion stewards in the earth, working in His deputized authority. Instead, they were toiling in their own strength to meet their own needs. This was not God being "mean." He was not punishing them or withholding from them. He did not remove them from Eden. They removed themselves. By their decisions. By not stewarding the realm of their soul. By choosing no longer to be three-in-one in the image of the Three-in-One.

Our original place of communion with God was in the Garden of Eden. Now, as New Testament believers, our place of communion with Him is in Christ. Because of Jesus, we have been re-created by the Creator (see 2 Corinthians 5:17). We are once again in the fullness of relationship with our heavenly Father, and once again His dominion stewards in the earth. In Christ, we once again dwell in the God-place, so that through us heaven can once again overlap earth, to the glory of the Lord.

The enemy still wants to sidle in with lies, half-truths and obfuscations that tempt us to choose to doubt and ultimately disobey God, so that we decide in our own free will to come out of the place of alignment, agreement, life, blessing and power. He knows God will never turn from us, so he works at getting us to turn from God. This shrewd, crafty and cunning enemy of ours has not changed. His tactics are the same. He still comes against our body and assaults our mind to get us to question whether God "really said" (see Genesis 3:1). He still wants us to believe something is missing or being denied to us, so that we will choose to decide for ourselves what is good or bad, as opposed to trusting in the goodness of God, the truth of His Word and the wisdom of His ways in all things at all times—especially when we do not understand or like our temporary circumstances. He will point to situations where we have experienced challenges in the past, have struggles in the present or have fear about our future. He wants us to choose to believe that God is keeping something from us, so that instead of operating from faith, choosing alignment and releasing light, life and blessings, we give in to fear, choose selfish rebellion and release darkness, death and curses.

All the enemy's efforts are ultimately focused on our soul—our place of decision. This is why it is critical for us to realize that as God's dominion stewards in the earth, the first realm we must steward and take authority over is ourselves. The more effective we are in stewarding the internal realm of our soul—watching over our mind, will and emotions so that we keep wholly in alignment with God's truth, will and ways—the more effective we will be in stewarding the external realms we are entrusted with.

Adam and Eve failed to steward their souls and themselves, which is why they came up short in stewarding the realm of the Garden. They chose to doubt God's word in their minds. They chose to eat of the apple with their bodies. They chose to desire forbidden fruit that would make them lords of their own lives—deciding for themselves what was good and what was evil—as opposed to trusting in the goodness and wisdom of God and what He said. The battle was in the soul then, and the battle is in the soul now.

What Will You Create?

The soul is the place where we make decisions and determine the course of our existence in the earth, and our impact on creation—alignment or rebellion, harmony or discord, life or death, blessing or curse, light and order, or darkness and chaos. The soul is where we choose. This can make it seem like the soul is "in charge," but it is not. Like all things of the Kingdom, the greatest among us is the servant to all (see Mark 9:34–35). The soul may have a great role in God's three-in-one divine design of us, but that role is to serve the fullness of who the Lord created us to be. The soul does this by being submitted to the leading of God through our born-again spirit and making faith-filled (and faith-fueled) decisions that keep our mind, heart and body (thoughts, feelings, words, actions and choices) in alignment and agreement with the truth of God's Word. It is the decisions you make in your soul that determine whether at any given moment you are communing with God or not—whether you are operating in dominion authority or selfish ambition.

As God's dominion steward in the earth, you are His answer to dealing with the darkness and chaos in the world today. You are made in His image and empowered to be His divine representative (His "re-presentation") throughout all of creation. In Genesis 1:1–25 God models to us how we can do this on His behalf and to His glory. He puts on display, for those of us who are made in His image, how we can operate in His divine authority in the earth.

When your body, soul and spirit flow in three-in-one agreement in the image of His Three-in-One unity, you can expect darkness to be shattered and chaos to be brought into divine order. When you choose to allow the true wisdom and revelation of your heavenly Father to lead you, body, soul and spirit, you become His gate through which heaven invades the earth. Jesus taught His disciples this, and that includes you (see Matthew 16:17–19).

The enemy knows this and is terrified of it. He is not your biggest problem; you are his. If you are willing to arise and shine—to stand with God and believe, no matter what— then there is no darkness, chaos, minion or manifestation of the enemy that will be able to stand before you (see Joshua 1:3–9).

That is why Satan wants to lure you into believing the lie that "something is missing" and that God is withholding something from you. Maybe it is a health situation. Maybe it is a financial one. Maybe it is a relationship challenge. Or maybe it is certain doors that just do not seem to be opening for you. But the bottom line is that the slithering snake will find something to hiss lies to you about in an attempt to get you up in your head, thinking, *Did God really say? Is that promise really true? Is it really for me?* He wants to get you to rebel against God by choosing fear instead of faith, doubt instead of determination or frustration instead of peace and rest.

The assault is on your soul, because that is the place where you will choose to believe or not, trust God or not. Your soul is where you will decide whether you will partake of all that God has declared is yours, or choose to take a bite out of something that looks good and makes sense, but goes against His truth. The enemy knows you are made in the image of the Creator and that because of that, you have the ability to make an impact on creation. That lying serpent does not want you bringing forth life, light, order and the Kingdom on earth through your bold and expectant faith in God and the truth of His Word. Instead, the enemy wants to lure you into choosing to be discouraged, depressed, disappointed and defeated, so that you release darkness, chaos and disorder. He knows you can bring forth blessings, so he wants to trick you into bringing forth curses instead.

The enemy always assaults the soul. His goal is to lure you into making the decision to believe something that is not in agreement with God's truth, so that your three-in-one is no longer in divine alignment. When your soul rises up and chooses to be out of agreement with the truth of God, it is like taking a bite out of the apple—you are deciding for yourself what is true, as opposed to choosing to trust in the truth of God. Your soul is taking charge and choosing to be "lord." In that moment, you are no longer in perfect union and communion with the Creator, and you have removed yourself from the "God-place" where heaven overlaps earth.

When you are out of divine order like this, it is not that you can no longer create; it is that what you create will no longer be in the image of God. It will no longer be of Him, for Him and like Him. Instead, it will be of fear, rebellion, doubt, pride, anger or some other *self*-ish agenda. In that moment, you are no longer choosing to be God's dominion steward in the earth, bringing forth light to all creation. You are choosing instead to be a pawn of Satan and a partner with darkness. The good news is that if you ever do choose to go to that out-of-alignment place, you can just as easily choose to come back into alignment. It is that simple.

The Power in a Change of Heart

Let me show you how powerful it is when you win the battle for your mind, will and emotions and choose to bring your body and your soul into alignment with the eternal truth of the Kingdom of God that fills and flows through your born-again spirit. A few years ago, I was at one of the most challenging points in my ten-year-plus battle of overcoming a mysterious and relentless attack of infirmity against my body. I often was too weak to stand or even sit up. Most of my days were spent lying on the couch. When I was able to get up and around to do some work or a few chores around the house, I was left weak and shaky for hours or even days afterward. My health and strength were at an all-time low. So was my attitude. But, as usual, God was willing to meet me exactly where I was and show me the divine power that is always available to us, no matter how we feel in our bodies or our souls, when we are willing to choose the eternal truth of His Kingdom over the report of our temporary circumstances.

So there I was, lying on the couch in the living room, not even able to keep my eyes open because of how my head burned and ached with yet another of my frequent fevers. All of a sudden I heard an odd sound. It was a sharp, solid, but also slightly muffled *thwump* just behind me. I opened my eyes and lifted myself up enough to turn and look. I saw an odd blurry mark on the plate-glass window of the sliding door that opened onto the patio outside. I pulled myself off the couch, took the few steps over to the door and sat down on the floor in front of it. As soon as I did, I could see what had made that sound and left the mark on the glass—a bird. A good-sized sparrow had flown at full speed into the door. It had splatted into the glass and fallen to the ground. I could see that its head was twisted around backward on its broken neck. It lay there on its back, still and lifeless, feet pointing straight up—almost like a caricature of a very dead bird.

I sat and stared at it for a minute or two, wondering what one does with a dead bird. There are a bunch of cats in our neighborhood, so I did not want to leave it there to be scavenged by one of them. But I also did not want to touch it, because I thought I remembered hearing somewhere in my past that wild birds can carry bugs, parasites or even diseases. The last thing I needed was to add some kind of "bird flu" to the long list of mysterious ailments I was already dealing with. I figured the best thing to do was to try to find a shovel in the garage to scoop up the bird and toss it into one of our big garbage cans.

That is when God spoke to my heart. In a still, small voice He invited me to pray for the bird. When He did, I immediately remembered the many times I had told Him how much I wanted to see and experience all the works Jesus did in the gospels—including the raising of the dead—just as He promises us in John 14:12. But that had been when I was traveling and preaching and ministering. That was when I had been stronger.

Again came His invitation to pray for the bird. So I did. Sitting there on the floor, from my side of the sliding glass door, I reached my hand out toward the bird and feebly prayed for that dead sparrow, which might well be infested with bird cooties that I did not want anything to do with. Nothing happened.

Then He spoke to my heart again and invited me to open the door and go outside. I reminded the Lord that with Him all things are possible, and that He was well able to reach out and do whatever it was He wanted to do for that bird as easily through a closed glass door as He could through an open glass door.

Loooooooong silence.

In that moment, I had a decision to make. Would I follow His leading, or would I follow my fear? It is a little embarrassing how long I sat there and wrestled with myself.

Eventually, I made my choice. I stood up, pulled back the sliding glass door and stepped out onto the patio. I knelt down near the bird and held my hand over it—probably a good eight to ten inches away. I began to pray in the name of Jesus for life to come back into the bird. It was still a somewhat halfhearted prayer, as what was really on my mind was to watch vigilantly and make sure no bugs or anything started jumping off the dead bird, looking for a new "host."

Again the Lord spoke to my heart. He invited me to pick up the bird. At that point I figured I had already come this far, having now entered the "hot zone" if there was one, so why not? I picked up the bird in my left hand. It was still. Lifeless. And its head was twisted back at that awful, broken-neck angle. It was on its back in my left palm, so I reached out and just barely touched it with my right index finger.

I do not remember exactly what I was praying. What I do remember is that shortly after touching that bird with my finger, the heart of the Father exploded in me. Compassion flooded into me, and all of a sudden I loved that bird. I loved that perfect little aspect of God's creation as fully and completely as the Creator Himself did. And I was brokenhearted that it was dead. I let go of all my fear and concerns and cradled that bird in my left hand while gently stroking it, almost petting it, with two of my right-hand fingers. I was no longer praying for the bird, but simply telling it how loved it was. All that I seemed to be able to speak over that wonderful little broken bird was how much God loved it. Again and again. I was lost in His massive and overwhelming heart for something that was incredibly dear to Him.

My heart was no longer closed off in fear, but wide open with love. My mind was no longer worrying about cooties or parasites; it was totally focused on releasing the fullness of God's passion. That was the moment when the sparrow's head snapped around, light came back into its eyes and it popped up and flew right out of my hand.

Stunned, I sat back on the patio. All I could think was *WOW!*

This vividly displays the divine power that is available to us in the earth to steward creation on God's behalf. When we choose to bring our souls and bodies into alignment and agreement with the reality of His Kingdom that our born-again spirits are always connected with, then we can fulfill our role as His agents of impact in the earth. It also reveals the ability, willingness and desire of God to lead us back into that place of alignment. The Lord met me exactly where I was. He did not disqualify me for the posture of my heart. He did not dismiss me for allowing myself to be mired temporarily in self-pity and fear. Just the opposite. He reached out with the right words and reminders all along the way. He helped me remember who I truly was. He encouraged me step by step, past every hesitation and resistance, back into that place of divine alignment and dominion power.

I had to choose to respond. I had to choose to follow His leading. I could have refused and just continued to lie there on the couch. I could have blamed God for not making it easier, especially after all I had been through and was already dealing with. I could have decided the bird was not important. After all, it was just one of dozens of sparrows that come to my backyard feeders every day. I could have made excuses and decided to dismiss His whispers as merely my imagination. I could have decided it was not worth the time and energy since I had never seen a dead bird raised before.

All those thoughts came into my head. All those feelings stirred in me. I had to decide to heed Him more than them. I had to be a dominion steward of the internal realm of my mind, will and emotions so that I could step into the place of being His dominion steward in the earth. For sure, I did not do it on my own. He led me step by step beyond my *self* every time there was a thought, feeling or decision that was about to stop me.

God will never force us to do anything, but He is willing to help us in everything. He leads—often in very subtle and almost missable ways. We choose whether or not to seek, look, listen and follow Him—whether or not to align our three-in-one with the Three-in-One. I choose, and you choose. Every moment of every day. When we choose to align with God, it opens the doors of heaven into the earth, and amazing things can happen.

We see a prophetic picture of this very thing with King David in 2 Samuel 6:1–19. At the beginning of this passage, King David desires to bring the Ark of the Lord—the living presence of the living God—back into his life, back into his city, back into his sphere of influence. He was excited and expectant. But then something happened that King David did not understand and did not like. It left him angry, afraid and confused. In that moment, he decided not to bring the Ark back into his sphere of influence, but instead to leave it behind. He chose to walk with confusion, fear and anger instead of continuing to walk with the presence and reality of God.

The Lord did not hold this against King David and give up on him. Just the opposite. The Lord found a way to stir the king's heart and reawaken his desire to walk with God and usher the glorious reality of the Lord's living presence back into all that he stewarded. King David decided to "change his mind." Now, despite what had happened, King David chose to let go of the past and grab hold of God.

Additionally, as he moved with the presence, he chose to stop every six steps to sacrifice an ox and a fatted calf unto the Lord, while also praising Him and dancing before Him with all his might. Six is the number that represents man (God made us on the sixth day). I believe that David making a sacrifice every six steps was a prophetic picture of how, whenever something in our *self*-ish nature tries to rise up and interfere with our walking with God, we must "kill the flesh" by choosing to rejoice in God. In other words, we choose to trust in the truth of God more than in the report of our circumstances, thoughts or feelings in any given moment.

There were still those things that King David did not understand or like, but he took dominion over his soul by choosing to praise God instead of being angry and afraid of Him. He took dominion over his body by choosing to dance before the Lord, as opposed to turning away from Him. He took dominion over his mind, will and emotions by choosing to align his thoughts, feelings and decisions with the truth of God. The result was that the living presence of the living God was ushered back into King David's sphere of influence, and the nation and its people were richly blessed.

Like He did with King David, the Lord has made you to rule and reign in the earth (see Genesis 1:26–28; Revelation 5:10). You are God's dominion steward over His creation. You are designed to walk with the Lord and release the reality of Him and His Kingdom into your sphere of influence, making the world a better place. When you choose to agree with this by deciding to align your three-in-one with the truth of the Three-in-One, you inhabit the glorious place where heaven overlaps earth through you as you manifest the presence and power of the One in whose image you are made. Maybe it is a bird being raised from the dead. Maybe it is a smile for someone who does not really deserve it. Maybe it is a kind word to your spouse when he or she has hurt or disappointed you. Maybe it is seeing your family, church, city or even your entire nation revived, reformed and radical for God. Whatever it is, you have the power in God to shift things in the earth by shifting them in yourself.

The first realm you steward is yourself. Others can do things or say things that are unkind, untrue or even unfair. Difficult, confusing and challenging times will come. These are all real things that have real impact. But what has even more impact than what happens to us is how we respond to those things. If we will maintain our place of authority by watching over the thoughts, emotions, decisions and actions we author and allow in response to what happens to us, we will stay in the place of alignment with God and be able to more effectively usher His presence, power and personality into our circumstances and our spheres of influence.

If you are willing to watch over the realm of your soul—taking responsibility for your mind, will and emotions—you will find that your thoughts, feelings and actions begin to align more and more with the divine nature of your heavenly Father, in whose image you have been remade by the gift of His Son and the leading of His Holy Spirit. The result will be an almost effortless manifestation of Him and His Kingdom into the earth.

Romans 8:19–21 says that all of creation is anxiously longing for and earnestly awaiting the manifestation of the sons of God. That word *sons* in the Greek is *huios*, and it means a mature one in relationship with God. These "sons" (men and women) are the ones who know they are made in His image. These are the ones who know who they are in Christ. They know who their Father is. And they choose to follow the leading of the Holy Spirit, as opposed to their old fallen nature. These are the ones who choose to deny fear and embrace faith, who refuse offense and choose love, who say no to despair and choose to rejoice, who maintain an eternal perspective in the midst of temporary circumstances, who face challenges by choosing to delight in the Lord, no matter what. These are the ones creation is eagerly anticipating. These "mature" ones know they have been set free from the curse, and they choose to live in that righteous freedom. From that place, they are able to be a powerful expression of the victory and goodness of God to all His creation.

Does that sound exciting? Does it stir something deep inside you as you read this? Of course it does. Because this is *you*. This is who you really are. You can do this! It is as simple as the choices you decide to make.

Choose to be who you truly are in Christ. Choose to bring your body and soul into alignment with the truth and freedom known deep-unto-deep in your born-again spirit. Choose to think and feel and act and decide in alignment with the heart of the Father and the mind of Christ, by the leading of the Holy Spirit. Choose to "arise and shine" as a harmonious three-in-one expression of our Three-in-One God, in whose image you were lovingly and powerfully made. And if you ever see that you have gotten out of unified three-in-one agreement with our Three-in-One God, choose to step back into it. Take dominion authority over the inner realm of your soul by stewarding your mind, will and emotions. As you do this more and more, you will see the Kingdom of God arise in you more and more. Creation will be affected as you shine His light, love and life out into the darkness (see Isaiah 60:1–3). Choose to be a mature "son of God," because when you make that choice, you bring heaven to earth. And in that, anything is possible.

Yes, the enemy will resist you, and at times so will your old carnal nature that still likes to try to be in charge. At times it is a battle. In truth, it is *the* battle. But here is the good news: It is not a battle you ever have to be afraid of. Because One came before you and won the battle for you. One who loves you. One who gave everything for you, so that you might enjoy the fullness of who He is and all that you were created for. All you need to do is agree with His truth and choose to live in His victory. He is so good that He will even help you with that.

Your Victory Is Certain

Let's go back to Adam and Eve for a moment. They did not win the battle for the mind, will and emotions in the Garden of Eden. You and I have also lost this battle at times. But the good news is that neither their mistakes nor ours took God by surprise or deterred Him from His plans. Before any of this ever happened, His perfect and victorious plan was already in place—the Lamb was slain before the foundation of the world was laid (see Ephesians 1:4–5; Revelation 13:8). Jesus Christ came to set us all free from our sins and bring us back into the fullness of relationship with Him. Through Christ and His finished work, we are once again fully His and fully empowered to be His beloved people—His dominion stewards in the earth.

You have been given more than just a "second chance." His mercies are new every single morning (see Lamentations 3:22–23). His forgiveness is total. His love is boundless. And His grace is unending. Every moment of every day, His great desire is to reach out with His great love and help you be a brilliant, shining "re-presentation" of Him to all creation. If you are in Christ, this is who you are! For He has won every battle for you, including the battle for the soul.

Satan tried the same thing with Jesus in the desert that he did with Adam and Eve in the Garden (see Matthew 4:1–11). Jesus, the Son of God, came as the Son of man to show the whole world the Father. He was the Father's perfect representative and representation in the earth (see John 14:7–9; Colossians 1:15; Hebrews 1:3). The first thing that Jesus did as He stepped out into His earthly ministry for the Father on our behalf was to allow the Holy Spirit to lead Him into the desert to win the battle for the soul that Adam and Eve lost in the Garden. After Jesus went forty days without food and water, the devil came and tempted Him to doubt the goodness of God based on His current circumstances. The devil tried to tempt Jesus to doubt His Sonship—His certain and secure relationship with His heavenly Father. The devil tried to tempt Him to choose to believe that something was missing, that something was lacking, that the Father was keeping something from Him.

"If You are the Son of God," that slithering snake hissed, "command that these stones become bread" (Matthew 4:3). The temptation was to let the volume of His circumstances (forty days without food or water) speak louder to Him than the truth of the certainty of the Father's love, wisdom and provision. If He gave in to that, He would allow His soul to rise up into a false position of lordship and choose to do what He was capable of (turn stones to bread, to provide for Himself in His earthy hunger), but it would be a rebellion against His Father.

Jesus' temptation was to use His authority in the earth to serve a selfish agenda instead of a divine one. It was the same temptation Adam and Eve gave in to. But not Jesus! His response was, "It is written, 'Man shall not live on bread alone, but on every word that proceeds out of the mouth of God'" (Matthew 4:4). What especially interests me about this declaration is that the last words that had proceeded from the mouth of God to Jesus were, "This is My beloved Son, in whom I am well-pleased" (Matthew 3:17). Jesus chose to trust in the fullness of that eternal truth—that declaration of certain love, acceptance and re-lationship—more than any temporary circumstance. Jesus, the Son of man, manifested in the earth on behalf of all men and women as a perfect three-in-one representation of our Three-in-One God (see John 14:9; Hebrews 1:3; Colossians 1:15). In doing this, He is not only our victorious Son-of-God Messiah, but also our glorious Son-of-man model for how to walk in the earth in the fullness of relationship with our heavenly Father (see John 14:12; 17:20–23; Romans 8:15–17, 29).

As the Son of man, on our behalf Jesus resisted the temptation to let an assault on His body tempt His soul to choose to rebel. He remained, as always, in divine alignment with the Father within His earthly body, soul and spirit. Jesus won the battle for the soul. Not for Himself. (After all, His soul is perfect.) But for each and every one of us, including you. This is why if we ever do allow ourselves to get "out of alignment" in our thoughts, feelings and decisions, we can just as easily choose to step back into the place of divine alignment and dominion authority. Jesus has made the way.

In Genesis 1, we see God as Three-in-One, acting in perfect harmony to bring forth all of creation, including us. He then placed us in the earth as His dominion stewards— created in His image to be His representatives. In the Garden of Eden, we lost this place and position through a battle of the soul when Adam and Eve made a bad choice based on wrong thoughts and selfish feelings. But Jesus came and won it all back for us. He won the battle of the soul on our behalf, just as He has won back our position and authority in God. The way we step into this victory is by choosing Jesus as Savior and also as Lord. We reenter the place of communion and empowerment by choosing, once again, to allow Christ to be the "head" (see Colossians 1:18–20) and by choosing for our body, soul and spirit to be fully His. We remain in this place of victory by choosing to trust in God and the eternal truth of His Word, no matter what. The battle takes place in our mind, will and emotions. As we choose to remain in Christ, we are certain to remain in victory.

BATTLE KEYS

Practical ways to apply the truths of this chapter in your life:

1. Read and meditate on Genesis 1:1–3. As you do, ask the Holy Spirit to reveal to you the immediate and transformative impact God the Creator has on darkness, disorder, chaos and areas of lack.

2. Remember that you are created in the image of God the Creator. You are empowered to be His dominion steward in the earth, and you are able, in His strength, to influence and affect creation with His light, life and love (see Genesis 1:26–27; John 14:12). Allow that truth to fill your mind and stir your faith.

3. Speak to any area of darkness, chaos, confusion or lack in your life, family, city or nation. Command that the light of God and the divine order of the Kingdom be established to usher in the reality of His goodness and the fullness of His blessing in every one of those areas.

4. Ask the Holy Spirit to reveal to you any time when you made wrong choices and decided to come out of agreement with the character and nature of God and the truth of His Word. Also ask what it was about that situation that seemed to speak louder to you than the truth of God. As the Holy Spirit reveals the root issue, ask Him to then go into that place and bring healing to it. By faith, receive His perfect love that casts out all fear (see 1 John 4:18).

5. Is there a place in your life right now that looks or feels as if there is lack or something missing? Ask the Lord to reveal His eternal truth to you in that situation. Receive a Scripture promise from Him. Stand on the eternal

truth of the Word by declaring it over and over again in faith every time you are tempted to believe your temporary circumstances, as opposed to the eternal truth.

6. Daily decrees for three-in-one unity:

- "I am made in the image of God."
- "My three parts—body, soul and spirit—are all in agreement with, and submitted to, the truth of God and the leading of His Holy Spirit."
- "I am a three-in-one expression of the fullness of God's goodness."
- "By the grace of God, the gift of His Son and the indwelling of the Holy Spirit, my body, soul and spirit cooperate in divine harmony to reveal the power and personality of God."
- "My born-again spirit is submitted to the truth of God in all things at all times."
- "I choose for my body to be submitted to the truth of God in all things at all times."
- "I choose for my soul to be submitted to the truth of God in all things at all times."
- "I am made in the image of God, and I make Him known everywhere I go, in every situation I find myself in."

2

A Divine Setup

This means that the things on earth will be shaken, so that only eternal things will be left.

Hebrews 12:27 NLT

God is good. His character and nature are good. Everything He authors and does is good. His promises are good. And, yes, even His processes that bring us into those promises are good. The bottom line is that God is very good, and very good at being God.

I often share with people that the most important decision we make, after deciding to say yes to Jesus as Lord, is to decide to trust that God is good. The reason this is so important is because if we know God is good, then we will look for and find His goodness in all that He does and all that He allows. No matter what. All the time. As it says in Romans 8:28, "God causes all things to work together for good to those who love God." That makes it really simple.

All things means *all* things. If we believe this, it will not only get us through the challenging times; it will get us looking for the goodness of God in those challenging times. It will get us seeking Him in expectation in those times, as opposed to turning away from Him in frustration.

When we know and trust in the goodness of God, it will spur us to be on the lookout for the blessing that is in the battle. This will help us steward our mind, will and emotions and keep them from getting out of control and leading us into places of fear, doubt, anger and frustration. It will keep us from rebelling and choosing to believe the report of a temporary challenge. Instead, we will stand strong on God's eternal truth, knowing that He is good and is well able to bring about the very best results from our current set of circumstances.

God established this in me early in my walk with Him. One of the very first promises the Lord ever highlighted to me was way back in early 2003, when I was a new believer. It was a night in the depths of the Montana winter. I was in my cabin, sitting in the big armchair by the woodstove. My Bible was in my lap, and I was having a conversation with Him. At one point, I felt stirred to ask Him for a promise Scripture—a word that I could lean on and count on and stand on as a "true truth" for me all my days. He whispered to my heart *Jeremiah 29:11*. I opened my paperback *NIV Men's Devotional Bible* to that passage and read: "'For I know the plans I have for you,' declares the LORD, 'plans to prosper you and not to harm you, plans to give you hope and a future.'"

I thanked Him for the word. I sat with it. I meditated on it. I mulled it over. I allowed it to go deep inside me as a foundational truth, just as I had asked. I let the word become mine. As I did, a question popped up in me. I asked the Lord, *Okay, I get the part about You wanting to prosper me, give me hope and bring me into all You created me for and have called me to. But what is the deal with the "not to harm me" part? Why did You word it that way? Why not just say You have "plans to prosper me—do good by me—and give me a hope and a future"? Why did You say "not to harm you"? I don't understand.*

Immediately, He spoke back to my heart that He worded it that way so that I would always know that His plans were never, ever to harm me—so if at any time I found myself in a situation that might look or feel that way, I could know it was not His intent to do harm. Just the opposite. It was, and always would be, His intent to do good—to use it all to prosper me and bring me into the future He has for me.

The same is true for you. He is good, and He is always working to bless you and bring you into the fullness of the glorious future He has created you for. The obvious blessings are, well, *obvious*. When you get that raise at work. When the house sells above asking price. When your prodigal gets the revelation and says yes to the Lord. When the refrigerator and pantry are stocked full of your favorite foods, and there is still plenty of money left in the checkbook to pay the month's bills. When you are surrounded by friends and family, all happy and healthy. When you find that great parking spot right in front of your appointment. And so many more.

But sometimes the blessings are not as immediately obvious. Sometimes, when God in His goodness is arranging things to bring about a deep desire of your heart, at first it might not look or feel like a blessing at all. It might look and feel like a battle or challenge. What it really is, though, is a divine setup—an opportunity God is presenting or allowing

that will bring you past a limitation and into a greater manifestation of His promises. Because remember, all that He is
and all that He has given us is ours in Christ. There is nothing of Himself or His Kingdom that He keeps from us. I am
not saying that we will ever be all that He is. Only God is
God. What I am saying is that the totality of His goodness
is ours in Christ. There is not one good thing of Him or His
Kingdom that we have not been given in the Son. God does
not keep any of His fullness from us, but sometimes in our
free will, we can unknowingly be keeping ourselves from that
fullness. In those areas, God in His goodness will often bring
us into a divine setup to help us see and get past anything in
us that is limiting, hindering or interfering with our walking in greater manifestations of all that is ours through the
complete gift of His Son.

Think of Martha, Mary and Lazarus in John 11. They
knew the Lord well. He had visited them many times. Martha had cooked for Him and served Him. Mary had sat
adoringly at His feet. Lazarus had shared many conversa-
tions with Him. They were friends. And even more than that,
they knew Jesus loved them. After all, when Lazarus became
seriously ill, the word they sent to Jesus was, "Lord, behold,
he whom You love is sick" (John 11:3).

Martha and Mary were confident in the goodness of
Jesus—so confident that they reached out to Him for help.
But then, when He did not respond the way they thought
He should, it caused them to start questioning that goodness. To their minds, if He truly cared, He would have come
right away. They did not understand why the Lord had not
immediately answered when they cried out to Him. They
were so upset by this that when Jesus did show up, Martha
buffeted Him with angry questions about why He had not

responded sooner, and Mary could not even bring herself to meet with Him at first (see John 11:20–32).

Did Jesus delay because He was not good? Did He tarry because He did not care? Did He hesitate because He had no solution? No. It was a divine setup. It was actually because He loved them so very much that the Lord responded according to His wisdom and timing, as opposed to theirs (see John 11:5–6). He knew it would be hard for them. He knew they would have to wrestle with some thoughts and emotions. But He also knew that it was all to bring them into something even greater than what they had reached out to Him for. These ones who loved Him and desired to know Him as fully as possible, these ones who had given all of themselves to Him whenever He was near, they were about to have the deep desire of their hearts to know Him more fully answered in a greater way than they had ever imagined. They knew Him as Lord. They knew Him as friend. They knew Him as lover of their souls. They even knew Him as healer. They were about to see all that and much more. But none of it would come about in the way (or in the timing) they expected. They would have to trust in His goodness, despite their circumstances. They would have to get their soul under control and win the battle for their mind, will and emotions, so that fear, frustration, anger and confusion did not cause them to turn away from God.

Martha and Mary chose to meet with the Lord in the midst of their heartache and questions. They chose to trust in His goodness, despite their circumstances. This opened the way for the Lord to move powerfully in their lives, and in the life of their brother, Lazarus, doing exceedingly and abundantly beyond what they had originally asked of Him. Lazarus not only was healed; he was raised from the dead. Martha, Mary and Lazarus were all greatly blessed as they each came to know the Lord in an even greater way than they had before. Plus, their whole community was affected—everyone in their sphere of influence saw the goodness of God and received a greater revelation of Jesus. What a lesson in the truth that if God seems to be taking longer than expected, it is simply because He is about to exceed our expectations.

One of the keys to winning the battle for your mind, will and emotions is never to let your circumstances affect your revelation of the goodness of God. Instead, allow your revelation of the goodness of God to affect your circumstances.

Shaking Things Up

We see this idea of a divine setup throughout Scripture. The story of Martha, Mary and Lazarus that we just discussed is one example. I believe the principle of this idea is revealed in Hebrews 12:26–27 and Haggai 2:6–9, when God talks about shaking things up so that something greater, deeper, more powerful and truer can come forth and be established. That is what a divine setup is all about—circumstances that God authors or allows that may not look or feel "divine" at first, but their purpose is to help us see wrong thoughts and feelings that fuel wrong responses. These wrong choices and reactions are almost always based on wrong systems of belief that were created because of trauma, disappointment, hurt, confusion and the like. They tend to be patterns of self-protection and self-defense, because for some reason in those circumstances, we have decided that we cannot trust God, but rather need to deal with things on our own.

Remember what we talked about in chapter 1. One of the main tactics of the enemy is to point to challenging circumstances and try to convince us that God's Word is not true, or is true for everyone else but us. The enemy wants us choosing to think and feel that God cannot be trusted or will not come through, so that we will choose to take things into our own hands—as opposed to trusting in, resting in and declaring the sure Word and victory of the Lord.

When we have a "self" pattern (self-defense, self-protection, self-righteousness, self-comfort, self-pity, self-reliance, selfishness) like this in our life, it is actually a "system" that we have allowed to become established in our soul. These systems can often be so ingrained in our thoughts, will and emotions that we are barely even aware of them. They make sense to our natural mind because of things we have seen (or not seen) and have been through, but as God lovingly and protectively declares over us in Proverbs 14:12 (emphasis added), "There is a way which *seems* right to a man, but its end is the way of death." Or to put it another way, the self-created and self-decided systems of *self* that we come up with on our own ultimately lead to self-destruction. This is why God will bring us into one divine setup after another to help us see the pattern, so that we choose to come out of agreement with the inferior system of *self* and allow the superior truth of His Kingdom to replace it.

Let's take a closer look at Hebrews 12:26–27. The New American Standard Bible translates the Greek this way:

> He has promised, saying, "Yet once more I will shake not only the earth, but also the heaven" . . . removing of those things which can be shaken, as of created things, so that those things which cannot be shaken may remain.

In the first part of this passage, the writer of Hebrews is referring back to a prophecy from Haggai, where God promises to shake earth and heaven. In the second part, the writer is helping New Testament believers understand what the Lord's purposes are in the shakings. God shakes things up to remove those things that are not His, so that they can be replaced with the unshakable, certain and eternal truth of Him and His Kingdom. God wants us to have a firm foundation. He wants us standing on divine truth, so that in any and every situation we are perfectly positioned for breakthrough and blessing. He will always arrange things to help us know, agree with, choose and inhabit the fullness of all He is, all He has done and all He has given us, all the time.

This passage is especially salient when we remember that the book of Hebrews was originally written to Jewish Christians who seemed to be wrestling with returning to some of the old ways of Judaism. God wanted them then—and wants us today—to know that no other systems or works are necessary. Jesus has done it all. No more acts are needed to earn favor with God. No more animals need to be sacrificed. No more penance has to be paid. There is no need to mix in elements of our old life, old ways, old thinking or old systems. Christ has come and given us all a new life. The Old Testament system of the Law has been completely fulfilled in Christ. Nothing is missing. No one who is in Christ is left out. We are holy by what He has done, not by anything we can do or add. God will move heaven and earth to help reveal the trap of a religious mindset, or any other wrong belief or thought pattern. Those ensnare us in a failed, performance-based reward system of self-effort and understanding, as opposed to His truth, which empowers us to inhabit victoriously the grace place of fully restored relationship and blessing through the imputed righteousness of our Messiah.

Shakings are one of the ways God helps us win the battle for our mind, will and emotions, so we can rest in Him and dwell in the promised land of all He has given us in Christ. The divine setup of His shakings helps reveal any inferior systems we have come into agreement with, so that they can be removed and replaced with His truth.

God's shakings are powerful, but they are rarely enjoyable. As a matter of fact, that word *shaken* in Hebrews 12:27 is *saleuo*, and it can also be translated as "agitate" or "disturb." Some of the agitating and disturbing things in our lives that we think are attacks of the enemy, or that we think are the fault of irritating people, are actually God's divine setups to show us that there is something in us that is not like Him. Something that is shakable. Something that is not rooted and grounded in the truth, character and nature of our Rock, Jesus Christ. These are mindsets and belief patterns that can keep us trapped in wrong thoughts, feelings and choices. They are lies that for some reason we are choosing to believe and buy into, often without even fully realizing it.

In His goodness, God wants to expose these things so that in our free will, we will choose to come out of agreement with them and instead grab hold of His truth, which leads to greater freedom and ultimately blessing. To accomplish this, He will sometimes allow us to be shaken through circumstances in our lives that disturb or agitate us. In that process, wrong thoughts, feelings, reactions and patterns pop up again and again, until we see them for what they are. His desire is not to make us feel guilty or ashamed. His desire is not to harm us. Just the opposite. His desire is that we will become aware of these things that hinder and interfere with our knowing the fullness of who we are in Christ, so that we will allow Him to root them out and replace them with eternal truth. His desire in the shakings, as in all things, is to use it all for our good.

In Haggai 2:6–9, a similar passage in the Old Testament, God also declares that He will shake all that can be shaken *so that* the latter glory of the Temple will be greater than the former, and there will be peace:

> For thus says the LORD of hosts, "Once more in a little while, I am going to shake the heavens and the earth, the sea also and the dry land. I will shake all the nations; and they will come with the wealth of all nations, and I will fill this house with glory," says the LORD of hosts. "The silver is Mine and the gold is Mine," declares the LORD of hosts. "The latter glory of this house will be greater than the former," says the LORD of hosts, "and in this place I will give peace," declares the LORD of hosts.

As New Testament believers, these are especially potent promises for us. God is the same yesterday, today and forever. The Temple, however, is not (see Malachi 3:6; Hebrews 13:8). The Temple where the Lord resides in the earth is no longer a building or a place; you and I are His temples. The eternal truth of this passage in Haggai about what God is like and what He does is as valid today as it was thousands of years ago. What has changed is that now, as New Testament believers, we clearly see that this eternal truth can be applied to each of us as the dwelling place of the Lord. God promises to shake whatever can be shaken. His purpose in this is so that anything that is old, outdated, not of eternal use or that does not serve us well will be revealed, dealt with and replaced with something that is much more glorious than the things of the world or of our old fallen, *self*-ish nature.

God's purpose is for His temples—you and me—to have a greater glory and be filled with His *shalom* (see Haggai 2:9). That Hebrew word *shalom* is usually translated as "peace," but it is actually so much more than what that one single English word can convey. *Shalom* is not merely a lack of stress or a time of tranquility. It is those things, but way more. In the Hebrew, *shalom* means peace, safety, happiness, well-being, health, prosperity, favor, rest and welfare—all in their totality. The *shalom* of God is the manifested fullness of all that He has done, all that He has given us and all that He has brought us into. Nothing missing. Nothing broken. Nothing out of alignment. Nothing less than His very best.

This, ultimately, is what the divine setup of His shakings is all about. Their purpose is to help us become aware of any systems, patterns or habitual thoughts, feelings and responses that are not of Him and are not the very best of the fullness He has given us. His shakings trigger those responses so we can clearly see them and come to discover why we are choosing to operate from them, as opposed to our true, born-again character and nature. Once we are aware of them, He helps us come out of agreement with them so that they can be removed and replaced by greater and more glorious manifestations of His truth. His desire is that we fully know and fully enjoy the fullness of His Kingdom within us.

Let's go back to Martha, Mary and Lazarus for a minute. When they reached out to the Lord for help in their time of need, they assumed He would respond right away. It probably never crossed their minds that their dear friend and beloved Lord would intentionally tarry for several days and wait to respond until after Lazarus had passed away—especially considering that the word of the Lord was that Lazarus's sickness would not end in death (see John 11:4). It would be easy to assume that this meant Lazarus would not die from his sickness, because the Lord would show up and heal him, just as Martha and Mary were expecting. But that was not the word of the Lord. The word of the Lord was that Lazarus's sickness would not *end* in death.

God always does exactly what He says, but He often does it in ways that do not make sense to us. This is because He is a good God who blesses us beyond our ability to ask, think or even comprehend (see 1 Corinthians 2:9; Ephesians 3:20). His promises are good. So are His processes. We usually can easily see the blessing in His promises when we receive them, but we often wrestle with seeing the blessing in His processes when we are in the midst of them. But the blessing is there. With Martha, Mary and Lazarus, it is very clear in Scripture why Jesus did what He did in the way that He did it. It was because He loved them, and so that the glory of God would be revealed (see John 11:4–5), just as He promises in the Hebrews 12 and Haggai 2 passages. The reason God authors or allows shakings is to help us get past something that is limiting us in some way, so that something more glorious can come forth and we can live in an even greater manifestation of the fullness of His goodness.

Martha and Mary were definitely shaken by the process they went through. As we saw, *shaken*, or *saleuo* in the Greek, is also translated as "agitate" or "disturb." They were shaken as they wrestled with fear, frustration, doubt and anger. They had to watch over and steward the inner realm of their soul. They had to decide whether or not they would allow those thoughts and feelings to control them, or whether they would control their thoughts and feelings. Ultimately, they won the battle for their mind, will and emotions. They did not allow wrong responses to keep them from Jesus. They chose, quite literally, to continue following Him, even to the place of their greatest confusion and disappointment—the tomb of their brother, Lazarus.

Because Mary and Martha did this, something greater and more glorious was revealed. The Lord absolutely kept His word. Lazarus's sickness did not end in death. It ended in a revelation of the no-matter-what resurrection power of God. Because they chose to continue turning to, talking with and following Jesus through the divine setup and shakings, even when they did not like or understand the process, they experienced a greater glory and came to know and trust Him more deeply and completely. Now they understood that He was not only their friend, healer, beloved, teacher and Lord, who would ultimately one day resurrect the dead at the end of time (see John 11:2–3, 21, 24, 27). He was also the God of the impossible, in whom all the I AM fullness is always present tense (see John 11:39–44). They now knew that there was nothing of the eternal realm of God that was only for a later day or in the sweet by-and-by. They now knew that the fullness of God was theirs in Christ all the time, no matter how things might look or feel along the way. Greater glory and *shalom*, indeed!

God hears every one of your prayers. He responds to every one of your requests. Just not always how, when, where or in the way you are expecting. This is because He is always working on multiple levels. We ask one thing, something that is really important to us, on which we are totally focused at the time. He responds in a way that not only addresses that current need, but also all our other prayers, requests, dreams and desires.

Don't forget, God is the Great I AM. He is always great. And He is always present tense. He is always working right now to bring about the fullness of all your hopes and your future (remember Jeremiah 29:11). We tend to focus on one thing at a time. When that thing does not seem to happen right away, it can trigger fear, doubt, anxiety, frustration and other negative thoughts and emotions. When that happens, remember that what we think of as disturbances and agitations are often actually the shakings of God. The purpose of His shakings is not to disturb or agitate you. Just the opposite. The purpose of His shakings is to help you become aware of any negative patterns in your thoughts, emotions and choices. In His goodness, He wants to help you see anywhere that you are believing, agreeing with or relying on an inferior system of *self*, as opposed to resting and trusting in Him and His eternal Kingdom.

When you do not understand what God is doing, do not despair. It is probably a divine setup. The process may not be easy, but it will be good, because He is good. If you have no idea what He is doing, it means He is arranging things to bring forth something exceedingly, abundantly beyond your ability to comprehend. It is all a divine setup so that the greater glory of the Kingdom that is already within you can be revealed, and so that you can live in a multiplied experience of His absolute *shalom*.

The Unshakable Kingdom Revealed

I have been an itinerant minister for many years. I have preached, prophesied, prayed and worked miracles in dozens of nations on almost every continent around the world. I have served the poor, the homeless and the drug addicted, as well as high-ranking officials and world leaders. I have ministered in churches, conferences, alleys, brothels, parliaments and more. It is a blessing to be one who brings the good news of the Gospel to the four corners of the earth. At times, it can also take a toll. All the miles. All the hours. All the airports. All the delays. All the demands. Preaching is a privilege and an honor. Traveling ministry is one of the main calls upon my life. It can also be a really good reminder that if I do not win the battle for my mind, will and emotions and choose to live from my born-again spirit, my flesh is just waiting to rise up.

A few years ago, I was in the midst of an especially busy season. I was also overcoming some ongoing health challenges, and I was not feeling very well. I was flying to conferences and events every week, with just enough time in between to land, drive home, do a load of laundry, check in with our team, repack and fly back out. And for some reason during this stretch, almost every flight I was on was either delayed, canceled or suffered equipment failures. I sat in airports. I sat on tarmacs. I missed connections. I had to reschedule things. Over and over. All due to no fault of my own. And wow, was it ever agitating and disturbing at times. I was getting frustrated. I was becoming cynical about airlines and customer service.

It all came to a head during a trip to England that summer, when there was one challenge after another. My flight out of Phoenix was delayed multiple times. When I arrived in London, my ride never showed up. There was a huge problem with the lodging I had arranged. And so on. It kept building up, until one day when I was headed from Central London to East London and then out to the coast. I realized I needed to reload my Oyster card (a smart card used to pay for public transportation throughout the greater London area) so I would be able to pay for all my rail transport. I used my credit card to top off my account with GBP 100 (about USD 150 at the time). The machine displayed that it was printing a receipt, but one never came out. I was in a hurry because I did not want to miss my train or the meeting I was scheduled to preach at that morning, but $150 is a lot of money to me. I needed a receipt. I talked to the ticket agent who was standing near the automatic machines and asked him if he could help me get a receipt. He very curtly said no.

Ooookay. I followed up with, "Can you tell me if there is any way for me to get a receipt?"

He told me, "You should have gotten your receipt from the machine."

Yes, I *should* have. That was the entire issue. I took a deep breath and started my explanation about the faulty machine all over again. I could feel tension building in me as I began to worry about how soon my train was due to depart.

The ticket agent pointed to a window on the other side of the automatic machines and told me, "You'll need to wait in line for the agent in the office. He might be able to help you."

That word *might* jumped out at me and triggered another surge of frustration. I let out a very dramatic sigh and headed over to the line. There were only two people ahead of me. I was hopeful, until I looked and saw that there was no one sitting at the desk behind the window. I asked the man in front of me, "Have you seen anyone in there?"

He told me in a very irritated voice (and in colorful language not included here), "There *was* someone back there, but he's been gone for a while now!"

I noticed the man in front of him was shifting back and forth and from side to side impatiently. Eventually, the agent behind the window showed up. The gentleman at the front of our line quickly moved toward the window, but was immediately told via a small loudspeaker to wait because he had not been called forward yet.

It was pretty clear that the ticket agent in the office was not having a great day and was in no hurry to be of any help to anyone. I looked up at the big board that listed all the train departure times. I had less than ten minutes to get to my train on the other side of the station. Frustration was building toward anger in me.

That is when the Lord spoke to me and asked, *What's going on with you?*

Right there in line, we had a conversation. I told Him, *I'm frustrated because I'm either going to miss my train and be late for my meeting, or I'm not going to get the receipt that I really need—which the machine was supposed to have given me already, by the way!*

He let me know, *I'm well aware of all that, but what's going on with YOU? Why are you allowing yourself to become so frustrated? Is it helping the situation?*

I took a deep breath and thought about His questions. *No,* I answered, *it for sure isn't helping. But . . .* And my thoughts trailed off. I was trying to express why it was all so irritating, but I could not quite find the words.

Always helpful, the Lord led me to the answer by asking, *Is it because you feel powerless?*

That's exactly it! I agreed. *I feel totally powerless. I either miss my train, or I don't get my receipt. And the one person who could help me is intentionally slowing everything down because he's having a bad day.* I felt I had no control over the situation—or any of the other travel situations that had delayed, hindered, agitated and disturbed me over the past several weeks. I did indeed feel very powerless.

That's a lie you're choosing to believe, the Lord spoke to me. *You're never powerless, because you always have power over yourself, your thoughts, your emotions and your reactions.*

As soon as He shared this, I saw it. We can never truly control what is going on around us. We cannot control other people. We cannot control planes or trains or ticket machines. We cannot control how fast a line moves or how helpful someone else is. But that does not mean we are powerless. We always have power over ourselves. I had not been stewarding the inner realm of my soul. I had not even been aware of—let alone been winning—the battle for my mind, will and emotions. I was letting my thoughts and feelings control me. My attitude had been, *You're darned right I'm irritated, because all of this is really irritating!*

But in that moment, the Lord helped me see the truth. I was irritated because I was choosing to be irritated. I was feeling powerless because I was not exercising power over myself. I felt like a victim of my circumstances because I was allowing myself to be a victim of my *self*-ish responses to those circumstances. I saw it all so clearly in that moment, but I still was not sure what to do. So I prayed one of my favorite and most frequent prayers: *Lord, help!*

The next thing that came to my mind was the truth of 2 Timothy 1:7: *God has not given me a spirit of fear, but one of love, power and self-control.* Sure, I might miss my train, or I might end up without a receipt and be out $150. But God and His Kingdom are bigger than all of that. There was nothing to be afraid of. There was no reason for me to continue choosing to be irritated, frustrated and feeling powerless. Just the opposite, actually. I had all the power I needed to take control—not of the situation per se, but of myself in the situation.

I took another deep breath, and by faith, as I exhaled, I released the lie and all the wrong thoughts and wrong emotions that had sprung from my agreement with it. I took self-control of the inner realm of my soul. At that moment, I chose to win the battle for my mind, will and emotions. I chose to rest in and trust in God and the eternal truth of His Word over the temporary challenges of my circumstances. I chose to stand on the unshakable Kingdom ground of the peace and confidence of Christ within me, who is the hope of glory in any and all situations. I chose to be a warrior, not a worrier; a victor, not a victim. I gave everything else over to the Lord.

It was now my turn to go up to the window. As I approached, I realized I was no longer tense, worried, frustrated or afraid. Actually, what I was feeling all of a sudden was concern for the ticket agent behind the window. He did not meet my eye when I stepped up to his station; he was busying himself with some papers in front of him.

I opened my mouth to speak, but instead of asking about my receipt, I asked him, "How is your day going?" I was amazed by the tenderness, patience and concern for him that was exuding out of me.

The agent was undone by it. He looked up, met my eye. And I watched as his guard visibly dropped and his attitude completely changed. He shared about some challenges he was dealing with.

I asked, "Could I say a quick prayer for you?"

He let me do that, and when I finished praying, he asked, "And how may I help you?"

Within a minute or two, I had a receipt and was on my way to my train, which I made with just a little time to spare.

I will not pretend that those months of travel challenges were not . . . well, challenging. But what I see now when I look back at it all are not the challenges, agitations and disturbances of the "shakings." I see the goodness of God, who, in His kindness, was allowing me to experience one divine setup after another to help me see a pattern of *self*-ish responses based on a disempowering lie that I had bought in to. He did it all so that the lie would be revealed, removed and replaced by His empowering, unshakable truth. The reason it took so long was not because God wanted to shake me over and over again. It was because God is unrelentingly good, ceaselessly kind and unyieldingly helpful. He pursued me with opportunity, until I was willing to let Him help me get past myself.

God wants us to live in the fullness of the blessing that is His Kingdom within us. He wants this for all of us, all the time. I do not want there to be any room for misunderstanding, so let me be very clear: The purpose of God's shakings is not so that you will be agitated and disturbed. His purpose is to help you see a *pattern* of being agitated and disturbed (or similar wrong responses), so that you can be set free. God shakes what can be shaken, so that His unshakable Kingdom that He has given you in its fullness can be revealed—not just to you, but for you.

If you find yourself consistently being shaken by your circumstances and responding with anger, frustration, self-pity, cynicism or similar negative attitudes, do not despair. You are amazingly close to a massive breakthrough. The fact that you now see the pattern is a huge part of your victory. The next step is to allow the Holy Spirit to reveal why. What shakable system of the world or the self have you been standing on? What lie based on temporary facts or circumstances have you bought into? And what unshakable Kingdom truth can you replace it with, so that even in the midst of challenging times, you are able to choose to inhabit the love, joy, peace, patience, kindness, goodness, faithfulness, gentleness and self-control that is Christ within you (see Galatians 5:22–25)? Do not forget, even when it looks and feels as if you do not have control over your circumstances, you still have control over your mind, will and emotions.

God's promise to you is that He will shake what can be shaken so that it can be replaced with something greater, more glorious and divinely certain. The shakings of God display His willingness to move heaven and earth so that you may know Him more fully and come into a deeper revelation and greater manifestation of all that He is, all that He has done and all that He has given you. God is good. And His purpose in any shakings He allows or authors in your life is to use them to bless and prosper you, to bring you into the fullness of your hopes and future.

We find a profound picture of this in Matthew 27:51–54, just after Jesus' final moments on the cross. Everything the Lord had done in the earth had built to this divine setup. He was dealing with every system of hell and death for our benefit. It was the greatest "shaking" of all time, so much so that the earth itself shook (see verse 51). The result of His shakings was that tombs gave up their dead, and the Roman centurion who had taken part in crucifying Jesus went from being a mocker and persecutor to a passionate believer. His eyes were opened to the truth, and he cried out a faith-filled declaration that truly Jesus was the Son of God. Life conquered death. Light shattered darkness. Truth triumphed over deception. The glorious One made way for that soldier—and for all of us—to receive a greater glory and know the fullness of Him and His peace. That is why God shakes what can be shaken. That is what His divine setups are all about.

BATTLE KEYS

Practical ways to apply the truths of this chapter in your life:

1. Declare the goodness of God. Whether or not your current circumstances look or feel good in the moment, God *is* good. Declaring this truth will remind you of that and bring you back into the faith place that He is well able to turn it all to the good. One of my favorite prayers and declarations in the midst of challenging times is, "God, thank You that You are good, and that You are well able to bring about the very best results from my current set of circumstances. I declare the fullness of Your goodness into all that I am facing. Thank You that You are at work, and that I will see the goodness of God in this season of my life."

2. Read and meditate on Jeremiah 29:11. Declare this eternal truth over yourself every day, until you know it is true for you and you are able to rest in the certainty that God is working all your circumstances to the good, and until you know He will use whatever you are facing to bring you into all that He created you for and called you to.

3. Decide (and declare) that your circumstances will not affect your revelation of the goodness of God, but that your revelation of the goodness of God will affect your circumstances.

4. Is there anywhere in your life where you are agitated or disturbed? Could it be the shaking of God? Do you see a pattern of wrong responses—fear, anger, frustration, self-pity, depression, defensiveness, anxiety, avoidance and the like—over a history of similar circumstances?

Or perhaps during difficult times, you see a pattern of relying on some form of self-comfort, whether it be food, sex, shopping, alcohol, drugs or something else, instead of relying on the Holy Spirit as your Comforter and a source of wisdom in how to better deal with the issues you are facing. If so, thank the Holy Spirit for helping you see the pattern. Then ask Him for His help and wisdom in stepping into the victory Jesus has given you over these issues. What lie have you been believing? What unshakable Kingdom truth can you replace that lie with? Come out of agreement with the lie and declare the truth over yourself. I recommend that you commit to declaring the truth/Scripture each morning when you wake up and each night when you go to bed. This will help you establish a new firm foundation of God's unshakable Kingdom in your life. If you find yourself being shaken again in this same area, declare Kingdom truth in that moment, and choose to think, feel and act from His truth, as opposed to from your flesh.

5. Remember that even when it looks and feels as if you have no control over your circumstances, you still have control over yourself. Do not let your thoughts and emotions rule over you, but instead, use these Battle Keys (and any others that the Holy Spirit may share with you) to rule over your thoughts and emotions.

3

"More" of God

His divine power has granted to us everything pertaining
to life and godliness . . . so that by them you may become
partakers of the divine nature.

2 Peter 1:3–4

Does all this talk about receiving a greater glory and
knowing the Lord in a greater way stir you? Are
you hungry for more of God? Have you ever cried
out, "More, Lord, more"? Or passionately prayed something
like, "O God, I must have more of You"? I am sure you have.
After all, you would not be reading this book (or all those
others that are probably lining your shelves and stacked up
on your bedside table) if you were not hungry for more of
God and His Kingdom.

I am hungry, too. Yet one of the things He has helped me
see is that we cannot actually have *more* of God. Not because
He does not want us to, but because He has already given us

everything through the gift of His Son. There is not one good thing missing. There is nothing He has held back from us. There is not one bit of His Kingdom we do not already have in Christ. Ephesians 1:3 clearly tells us that God *has blessed us* with *every* spiritual blessing in heavenly places in Christ.

Did you catch that? Not *He will* bless us one day, when we cross over into heaven. Not *He might* give us some blessings some of the time. Not *if we do more*, He will give us more. No. God promises us in His Word that He has blessed us in Christ with every good gift, and with all the fruit and gifts of the Holy Spirit. It is done. That means if we are in Christ, we have the fullness of God right here, right now. Or, as the apostle Peter put it when he was mentoring believers to stand in the truth no matter what was going on around them in the earth or in their lives, when we know Jesus, we can be confident that God in His divine power has given us everything pertaining to life and godliness, and we can partake of His divine nature (see 2 Peter 1:2–4). Just as in Ephesians 1:3 we see that this fullness is not for one day off in the future or in the sweet by-and-by, but that this fullness of *all things* and the ability to partake of His *divine nature has been given to us already* in Christ.

Even though that impassioned cry of our hearts for *more* of God is technically theologically inaccurate, the Lord still loves it because He knows that what we are really crying out for is a greater manifestation of all that we know is ours in Him. Actually, that is why we hunger so deeply and cry out so passionately—we *know* it is ours! And we want to see it. He loves that. It is His great desire for us to live in the fullness of all He *has given* us.

When you said yes to Jesus as your Lord and Savior, your born-again spirit received the fullness of God, all He has done and all He has given (see Psalm 84:11–12; Romans 8:32; 2 Corinthians 5:17; Ephesians 1:23). All your sins are forgiven (see Luke 7:48, 50). This not only means that your record is wiped clean and you will not go to hell; it also means that everything that separated you from the Holy One and barred you from dwelling in the reality of "on earth as it is in heaven" has been dealt with on your behalf. The Son of God became the Son of man so that you, and every other child of man, could become a child of God. Jesus has done it all, and in that, He has given you all—all of His Father, all of His Holy Spirit and all of His Kingdom—right here, right now, on earth. You are completely, utterly and totally restored to relationship with God (see John 17:22; Romans 8:15–17). Nothing is missing. Your born-again spirit dwells in the reality of this fullness every moment of every day. That is why you are so hungry to see more of it made manifest. Because your born-again spirit knows it is yours.

Imagine if you went to your bank to withdraw $10,000, and the teller told you it was not possible because you had a zero balance. If you knew it was true—that there really was no money in your account—you would probably shrug your shoulders and walk away. But what if you knew it was a lie? What if you knew you had that amount, and much more, in your account? That would be different, would it not? You would be quite passionate about getting your money, would you not? Of course you would. And if you would be passionately stirred in regard to the riches of this world, is it any wonder your soul cries out so intensely at times for the true riches of the Kingdom, which your born-again spirit knows Jesus has placed into your account for you?

I know this eternal truth of having already been given the fullness of the Kingdom can be a hard thing for us to get our head around at times, especially when we are in the midst of ongoing circumstances that seem to scream at us to the contrary. But bluntly, part of the challenge is that too often we let our head lead based on what we have seen (or not seen), as opposed to living from our born-again spirit that knows the no-matter-what truth that we *have been* given everything in Christ—that it *is* ours. And I understand just how hard it can be. I have wrestled with it at times myself. This is the battle for the mind, will and emotions. It is what the enemy and his minions count on and stoke. They are always working to tempt us to let our head and heart lead. They want us living (and thinking and feeling and making decisions) based on the appearance of temporary facts, as opposed to the certainty of eternal truth. This has been their main push ever since the Garden of Eden, when Satan convinced Adam and Eve that God was holding out on them. The enemy goaded them to rebel against the word of God and decide for themselves what was best, based on how things looked, felt and seemed in that moment.

This is still one of hell's big guns against believers. It is why God declares in multiple places throughout His Word that when we are made right and restored to relationship with Him, the key to living in the totality of all we have in Christ through His imputed righteousness is to live by faith, not by feelings (see Habakkuk 2:4; Romans 1:17; Galatians 3:11; Hebrews 10:38). That word *live* in the New Testament Greek is *zao*, which can also be translated as "quick." The word *quicken* in Romans 8:11, where it promises that the Holy Spirit is at work within us and will make us *fully* alive, is derived from that same word. In other words, the key to us living in the fullness we have in Christ is to believe in that fullness. Our faith in His eternal truth over any temporary circumstances is actually what helps quicken and manifest in the natural that which we know is ours in the spirit.

The apostle Paul focused on this when he was mentoring believers during the establishment of the miracle-working Church of first-century Christianity. The early Church believers went forth and changed the world by putting the reality of the Kingdom within them on display. In his letter to the church at Ephesus, Paul reminds them all that we, as believers in Christ, have been given everything of the Kingdom (see Ephesians 1:3–8). He then goes on to say that his constant prayer is that they would know and understand the "rich and glorious" fullness God "has given" them and all His people (Ephesians 1:18 NLT; see also verses 15–18). Paul prays that the believers' hearts and minds (i.e., their feelings and thoughts) would be flooded with the reality of this truth, because incredible power comes from knowing and choosing to believe that God *has* filled us all-in-all with His Spirit through His Son. It is a power in Christ over all things (see verses 19–23). The key is choosing to believe it. Our born-again spirit urges us toward that choice, but ultimately, it is made in the realm of our soul.

The Holy Spirit intercedes for you and all believers today with even more passion than the apostle Paul prayed with for the church at Ephesus (see Romans 8:26). God loves your cry for *more*. He is stirring that hunger inside you so that you cry out, asking for the greater manifestations of what your spirit knows is yours. When you do that, you are actually crying out to God for His divine setups. You are asking Him to help you get beyond anything that keeps you from agreeing with the fullness of His Kingdom that you have been given. Your cry for *More, Lord!* really is the cry of *I must decrease so that He, and all of Him that is within me, may increase.*

Or to put it in the context of all we have been talking about so far, *Lord, send Your shakings to reveal and replace any mindsets or belief patterns that limit me from agreeing with and walking in the fullness of all You have given me in Christ.*

It is just a lot easier and a lot quicker to cry out, *More, Lord!* But what it all boils down to is a free-will request in which we ask God to help us get out of our own way. Amen!

Revival Begins Within

We were originally created by fullness, in fullness, for fullness. That is how our Three-in-One God made us in His image, to be His dominion representatives who steward creation on behalf of Him and His Kingdom (see Genesis 1:26–28). After the fall, God's plan for us to walk in divine fullness did not change. The Father sent the Son so we could be filled with His Holy Spirit and could once again inhabit the all-in-all place of restored relationship, operating with Him and for Him to advance His Kingdom in the earth.

Jesus did it all so we could have it all, because the Father loves all and the Holy Spirit will fill all. This is the good news of the Gospel. If we are in Christ, we have it. It is finished, done, complete. Jesus said so in John 19:30. The word in Greek that He declares on the cross when He says "It is finished!" is *teleo*, and its meaning is not only "finished, concluded and accomplished." Its meaning is also "to fill up." Peter, Paul and most importantly the Lord Himself tell us that He has given us everything. Nothing is missing. Nothing is held back. That is eternal truth. No matter how it might look or feel at any given moment.

As we talked about in the previous chapter, God will bless us with one divine setup after another to reveal and ultimately replace any wrong belief systems or behavior patterns that get in the way of our seeing and agreeing with His eternal truth, above and beyond any temporal circumstances. The way we dwell in and operate from the fullness we have in Christ is by choosing to believe it.

This is how every great move of God begins in the earth—believers deciding to believe the eternal truth of God above any temporary circumstances in their lives, families, cities, nations or regions that would seem to contradict it. Revival begins within. When we choose to trust God and His Word above all else—including our own understanding—we make place for the truth of His Word to be made manifest in notable and remarkable ways.

Every move of God in the earth begins not just *with* believers, but *in* believers, when we win the battle for our mind, will and emotions and choose to believe the Word of the Lord, no matter what, because we have decided it is more real and more true than anything else we might think or feel. Our decision to believe is the substance of faith that manifests the Word of the Lord that we know is absolutely true for no other "rational" reason than the fact that God said it.

Get Control of Your Soul

God's divine setups help us see anywhere that our mind, will and emotions are out of alignment with the truth that our born-again spirit knows. The setups are His way of getting us past anything that might hinder, limit or interfere with us walking in greater dominion authority and increased expressions of His presence, power and personality. Pentecost is a powerful example of this. We all know what happened on the Day of Pentecost. The Kingdom of God broke forth and empowered His New Testament Church to go out and change the world. On that day alone, three thousand were saved and baptized because of the reality of the Kingdom that was put on display through the believers (see Acts 2:1–4, 41).

What happened at Pentecost is powerful and important. So is what happened during the days that preceded it. As modern-day believers, we can learn a lot from how the Lord led Peter, James, John and His other original disciples to be part of the 120 gathered in the Upper Room that day. Let's start back in John 20. At this point in the gospels, those guys are pretty freaked out. Nothing has gone the way they thought it would. The Lord had clearly explained what was going to happen, including His arrest, trial, death and resurrection (see Matthew 16:21). Despite His explanation, however, they were still leaning on their own understanding of the events that had occurred over the last few days. They were confused, scared, disappointed and basically losing the battle for their mind, will and emotions on every front. According to John 20:19, they were literally locked up in fear, hiding behind bolted doors out of concern that the Jewish leaders would come against them, as they had come against Jesus.

This is when the Risen Lord shows up. As He stands in their midst, He declares, "Peace be with you," and then He shows them His hands and His side (see verses 19–20). That word *peace* that He declares is *eirene* in the Greek. One of the ways it can be translated is "the blessed state of a devout and upright man after death." In other words, what the victorious Risen Lord is saying and releasing to them is the grace to die to themselves—die to fear, confusion, disappointment, self-protection—so that they can move beyond the limitations of *self* and step into the fullness of the Kingdom that He gave His life for them to have. Jesus helps them realize that the only thing getting in their way is *them*. He helps them see that the Jewish leaders are not their biggest problem; they are their own biggest problem. He points out to them the importance of winning the battle for their mind, will and emotions, while also letting them know that they are not alone in the battle. He is right there with them, making available to them all they will need to get their soul under control and step out of fear into victory.

After extending the invitation of *eirene* to them, Jesus put the reality of His love on display for all to see. He showed them the wounds in His hands and side. He showed them that there was nothing He would not do, and nothing He had not done to meet all their needs, all the time. They went from being filled with fear to being filled with joy (see John 20:19–20). This positioned them to walk in divine empowerment as they each received the gift of His Holy Spirit (see verse 22).

The word for the *joy* that they were filled with is *chairo* in the Greek, and it can be translated as "glad," "calmly happy," or even "farewell." In that moment, Jesus the Risen Lord helps the disciples see that His love for them, and His ability to make a way when there seems to be no way, is always bigger and more powerful than any challenge or battle they might find themselves in, no matter how confusing or overwhelming it might seem. Choosing to get our eyes off our problems and onto Him—focusing on His love for us and all He has done for us in that love—empowers us to go from being freaked out to being calmly happy and filled with joyful expectation. We can say farewell to fear and step back into faith. We can stop being a victim of our circumstances, and become a victor in our circumstances. We can go from being pitiful to being powerful.

We see in John 20:19 one of the very first things the Risen Lord did when He appeared to His disciples was to mentor them in how to win the battle for their mind, will and emotions. This began five and a half weeks of Jesus teaching the disciples, all leading up to one of the most important and empowering divine setups ever—the ten days preceding Pentecost.

During the forty days after His resurrection, the Risen Lord appeared to the disciples to talk with them, teach them and mentor them about the new realm He had made available to them (see Acts 1:1–8). During these times, He "proved to them in many ways that He was actually alive. And He talked to them about the Kingdom of God" (Acts 1:3 NLT). He was helping the disciples see that everything had changed for them. Hell, sin and death had been defeated; all things were truly possible with God; the fallen flesh had been overcome; and they were fully restored to relationship with their heavenly Father. They could now once again be His dominion stewards and representatives in the earth.

Jesus wanted the disciples to see that they were now part of a new realm—in the earth but no longer of it. They were no longer fallen and separated from God, but were once again united with Him and empowered by Him. Jesus wanted them to realize that all He had told them during that last Passover meal they had shared together in Jerusalem was now theirs, including doing the works that He had done and even greater works (see John 14:12). He wanted them to realize that the reason they had not understood what He was doing at the cross was because He was accomplishing something bigger than their understanding. It was something exceedingly, abundantly beyond their ability to ask, think or comprehend, and it was now theirs. He was opening their eyes to the reality that because He was the victorious Messiah, they could now move in all He had modeled to them when He had walked the earth with them. He was letting them know He had done it all and had given them everything. All of this led up to an invitation to tarry in Jerusalem for a few days and wait for the promise of the Father (see Luke 24:49; Acts 1:4).

So the Risen Lord spends the better part of six weeks appearing to the disciples, teaching them, mentoring them and opening their minds to all that He has done, all that He has made available to them, all that is now theirs. But then He tops it all off with an invitation to tarry for a few days and wait. Why? Because it was a divine setup! God, in His infinite goodness and wisdom, was blessing them with the opportunity to decide whether or not they truly believed all He had done, all He had given them and all He had said.

If you have read the Bible, you know it was a ten-day wait until Pentecost. But the disciples did not know it. They just knew He said to wait, to tarry for a few days. Those ten days were more than enough time for issues, questions and concerns to come up in each of the disciples. Peter, James and John had not been able to tarry for one hour in prayer back when Jesus had been in the Garden of Gethsemane and had asked them to stand with Him and intercede (see Matthew 26:40). Now they were looking at an indeterminate amount of time.

I guarantee that issues of impatience, doubt, confusion, anxiety and fear came up in each of the disciples over those ten days. There are times in the middle of the night when the Lord will wake me and whisper an invitation to my heart, asking me to come and spend time with Him in my prayer chair. At times I have gotten up and then wrestled with wanting to go back to sleep when it did not look or feel as if He showed up within ten minutes, let alone ten days. So put yourself in their shoes. They have this incredible series of face-to-face visitations with the Risen Lord, and He tells them all that is now theirs. Then He lets them know that the key to stepping into it all is to tarry in the Upper Room and wait for a bit. I am sure their zeal and excitement carried them through the first day or two. But then three days, and four. Nothing. Five days, and six. Zip. Then a week. Then more than a week. Then a bunch more than a week. And still nothing.

Doubt had to be dealt with. Tempers may have even flared. Had they missed it? Was it ever going to happen? Was one of the others doing something wrong and blocking everyone else's blessing? Did God *really* say? They had to win the battle for their mind, will and emotions and get their soul under control—which was the exact point of the divine setup. Remember what we learned in chapter 2: God will shake what can be shaken *so that* His unshakable Kingdom will remain (see Hebrews 12:26–27).

Those ten days were a blessed time of opportunity when the disciples got to decide what they really believed. Was it the word of the Lord, or how things looked and felt? Each of them got to choose faith over fear—again and again. The kingdom of *self* was shaken over those ten days, so that the Kingdom of God could be revealed. And wow, was it ever revealed! On the tenth day, the Holy Spirit exploded into that place and fulfilled every single word the Risen Lord had spoken to them.

Remember, the disciples who had been behind those locked doors with the Risen Lord in John 20:19 had already received His Holy Spirit (see John 20:22). They were filled. But now, after going through the shakings of that ten-day divine setup and winning the battle for their mind, will and emotions, they were moving in the power of the Holy Spirit. Jesus, the Son of God, modeled this principle to us when He was in the earth as the Son of man. After His baptism, He was filled with the Spirit. He was then led *by the Holy Spirit* into the desert to be tempted by Satan (see Luke 3:21–22; 4:1–2). This was a divine setup. During that time in the desert, Jesus, whose soul was perfect, won the battle for the mind, will and emotions on our behalf (just as He was baptized on our behalf). The result was He came out of the desert in the power of the Holy Spirit (see Luke 4:14).

Over those ten days leading up to Pentecost, the Lord was teaching His disciples that the first realm we must learn to steward in dominion authority is the realm of our mind, will and emotions. What was true for them then is just as true for you and me now. Revival begins within. Your soul is the place of volition. It is where you decide what you really believe. Is it the eternal truth of God's Word, or how things look and feel at any given moment? Just like the disciples, when you choose to trust God again and again, no matter what—when you win the battle for your mind, will and emotions—you position yourself to operate in a multiplied manifestation of His presence, power and personality.

BATTLE KEYS

Practical ways to apply the truths of this chapter in your life:

1. Be a partaker of God's divine nature. Meditate on Scriptures like Ephesians 1:3 and 2 Peter 1:2–4. Ask the Holy

Spirit to help you realize that you have already been given everything in Christ. As you allow this eternal truth to become more and more of a certainty to you, you will be able to partake of His divine nature more and more. Think of an area you wrestle with the most, for example patience. The next time you feel impatient, realize that it is not that you need more patience from God to be a more patient person. God has already given you the fullness of His patience. So declare over yourself multiple times a day that you *are* patient. Then from this truth, choose to partake more often of the fullness of patience you have been given. It is the same with love, joy, peace, kindness, self-control and every other aspect of His divine character and nature. You do not need more of any of them (because you have been given all of them in fullness in Christ, through the Holy Spirit). You simply need to choose more often to partake of God's divine nature, the fullness of which you have already received.

2. Focus on the positive. In Matthew 16:21–23, when Jesus told the disciples what would happen when they all went to Jerusalem together, Peter focused on the parts about Jesus suffering, being arrested and killed, instead of focusing on the miraculously good news that Jesus would be raised from the dead. Challenges are challenging, but there is always good news when we are walking with Jesus. In your difficult times, ask the Lord to help you see some of the good things in your life that He has blessed you with. This will do two things that will hearten you: First, you will be connecting with Him. Second, it will give you something positive to focus on. Fill your thoughts and emotions with the good things

of God and of your life in the challenging times, and you will be amazed at how it will stir faith, hope and expectation for the good God will bring forth.

3. By faith, receive the peace/*eirene* of the Risen Lord to help you die to self and come fully alive in Him. Tell Him, *Lord Jesus, by faith I receive Your* eirene. *Right here, right now, I remember the wounds You bore and the price You paid for me to walk in victory always. I remember that You care for me even more than I care for myself. I thank You, Risen Lord, that Your peace/* eirene *is filling me now and giving me the grace to die to myself. I die to fear. I die to anxiety. I die to impatience. I die to irritation. I die to the need to understand. I die to anything and everything else that would lock me up in wrong responses. Instead, I come fully alive in You. My mind is off myself, off my circumstances and completely focused on You—my victorious Risen Lord. As I do this, I also by faith receive a fresh filling of the Holy Spirit from You. Breathe upon me, Lord, and fill me afresh with Your presence, power and personality.*

4

The Power of Your Mind

Whatsoever things are true, whatsoever things are honest, whatsoever things are just, whatsoever things are pure, whatsoever things are lovely, whatsoever things are of good report . . . think on these things.

Philippians 4:8 KJV

In 1637, the philosopher René Descartes laid one of the cornerstones of Western thought when he put forth his proposition "I think, therefore I am." What he was positing was that the very fact that we think proves we exist. Another way he put it was that "we cannot doubt of our existence while we doubt." This idea of thinking thoughts being proof that we are not simply dreaming or imagining existence, but that we do actually exist, became known as "the cogito," and from the seventeenth century on, it helped exalt the mind in Western society. In the last decade, medical and scientific evidence is showing that our mind and the thoughts we think go well beyond simply being proof we exist; they actually shape our existence and determine our reality.

As anyone who has read the Bible knows, the Word of God was way ahead of the curve on this. Proverbs, also known as the Book of Wisdom, tells us exactly what medical science is now discovering—that as a person "thinks in his heart [soul], so is he" (Proverbs 23:7 NKJV). The word *thinks* there is *sha'ar* in the Hebrew, and one of its meanings is "to act as a gatekeeper." This is why it is key that we win the battle for our mind. The thoughts we allow—the things we dwell on— are more than just simple musings. Our mind is a "gate," and the thoughts that pass through it affect us on multiple, very real levels.

Before we go any further, let's take a minute to discuss the difference between the mind and the brain. Those words are often used almost interchangeably, but they are actually two different things. Your brain is an organ that is part of your physical body. It controls your bodily functions. Your mind is an aspect of your soul, and it is what controls your brain. You can think of it as your physical brain being the computer hardware, and your mind being the software operating system that runs the computer. Your brain directs the body. Your mind directs the brain. That means that your mind has a huge influence on your health and well-being, your energy levels, your mood, your outlook, your productivity—*your life*! Because just as it says in Proverbs 23:7, as you think, so you are.

The thoughts we allow in our mind drive our brain, which then drives our body. Our mind has the capacity to affect our behavior and determine how we feel emotionally and physically. That not only has an impact on us, but also on the people and places around us. If we are thinking positive, happy, faith-filled, Kingdom-minded thoughts, it will be reflected on our face and in our posture, our energy level, how we interact with others and multiple other ways. To the contrary, if we allow the "gate" of our mind to be filled with negative, bitter, angry, dark, disappointed, offended thoughts, what we release into our body and into the world around us will be very different.

This is not just supposition. Science is catching up to the Word of God and revealing that many mental, emotional and physical illnesses are as much (or more) influenced by our thoughts as they are by our genes and physical environment. In her book *Switch on Your Brain* (Baker, 2015), Dr. Caroline Leaf, a pioneer in cognitive neuroscience for more than thirty years, cites research suggesting that as much as 75–98 percent of mental, physical and behavioral illness can be traced back to our thought life (see page 33). A field of science called epigenetics studies the effects that outside influences have on our genes. We have long known that things like a healthy diet and exercise can positively affect us, and conversely that a poor diet and lack of exercise have the potential to negatively affect us. But what is fascinating is that many studies now seem to indicate that positive and negative thoughts can have as much or more of an impact on our genes as other external influences like diet and exercise.

Here is a really simple example of how the thoughts we allow in our head can impact us physically and emotionally: A couple of years ago, when we started Shiloh Fellowship, we needed pictures of the apostolic leaders for our church webpage. This was before I was doing much media and television, and I tended to get a bit self-conscious whenever a camera was pointed at me. When it came time for the photo shoot, I immediately got up in my head, thinking about how I do not like to have my picture taken, how it always feels so staged and forced and how I never really take a good picture. All of this was making me quite self-conscious. I was filling my mind with thoughts about how unnatural the whole process of posing for a photo seemed to me. Of course, the initial result was that I was looking very posed and unnatural. I kept thinking about what to do with my hands. I was trying to figure out how big a smile I should smile. I was all locked up.

The photographer noticed how uncomfortable I was, and just before she took the next series of shots, she quietly said, "Think about your wife."

It was brilliant. As soon as she said that, I got my mind totally off the camera and myself. My thoughts went from self-fulfilling prophecies of *I never take a good picture* to thinking about how much I love and enjoy my wonderful wife. When I "changed my mind," everything else changed, too. A genuine, warm, real smile spread across my face. My eyes filled with light. And we got some really good photos.

Watch Your Focus

The only thing that changed during that photo shoot was the kind of thoughts I allowed to fill my mind. The lighting did not change. The backdrop did not change. My clothes did not change. The photographer did not change. The camera did not change. My thoughts changed. And that shifted everything.

As my dear friend and mentor Patricia King always says, "Whatever we focus on, we empower." If we focus on negative things, we empower negativity in our life. If we focus on dark things, we empower darkness in our life. If we focus on selfish and carnal things, we empower our fallen nature. If we murmur, complain and focus on how unfair everything seems to be in a difficult situation, we are not helping resolve the issue. Instead, we are actually empowering more frustration, anger, bitterness, disappointment and injustice in our life. If we choose to focus on Kingdom truth, however, then we empower the love, light and life of Jesus to fill us and flow through us to the world around us.

The apostle Paul said the same thing when mentoring believers in Philippi:

> Whatsoever things are true, whatsoever things are honest, whatsoever things are just, whatsoever things are pure, whatsoever things are lovely, whatsoever things are of good report . . . think on these things.
>
> Philippians 4:8 KJV

The amazing thing about this is that Paul wrote his letter to the Philippians from prison. He was locked up in awful conditions, not sure if he would live or die. Yet he wrote again and again about things like joy, rejoicing, eager expectation, the privilege of walking with Christ, hope, confidence and peace. Near the end of his letter, he shared how this is all possible—by choosing what we focus on. By deciding what we think about. By filling our mind with thoughts that are "true . . . honest . . . pure . . . lovely . . . good." Paul was spelling it out for the Philippians, and for all of us: If we choose to focus our mind on good things, we will empower good things in our lives. If we watch over the realm of our soul, choosing to be dominion stewards of our thoughts, we create an atmosphere of love, light and life. It begins with us, and then passes through the gate of our mind, into our body and out into the world.

Paul was locked up in horrible conditions, but he chose to think about all the good in his life. This not only shifted things for him; it allowed him to release good to others. What we focus on, we empower. What we fill our mind with becomes our reality. So even if, in the midst of temporarily challenging circumstances, we choose to focus on the good in our lives, we will establish a realm of goodness that becomes our "atmosphere." And there is always good in our lives, because the Kingdom of God is good and dwells within us. Despite how "everything" might look and feel in any given moment, the truth is that if we are in Christ, then we always have a realm of good that we can tap into. By focusing on that, by dwelling on that, by filling our mind with that, we will change our reality. The Word of God says so. And more and more, the world of science is discovering and declaring this truth as well.

Take Every Thought Captive

Let's dig into this a little bit more by looking at another passage from one of the apostle Paul's letters written while he was a prisoner in that Roman jail. In his epistle to the Colossians, Paul not only again talks about the importance of what we let our mind be filled with; he also gives a key to how and why we can always find good to focus on:

> Since you have been raised to new life with Christ, set your sights on the realities of heaven, where Christ sits at God's right hand in the place of honor and power. Let heaven fill your thoughts. Do not think only about things down here on earth.
>
> Colossians 3:1–2 NLT

It all begins with realizing, focusing on and agreeing with the truth that we have been raised up by Christ into a *new* life. We are new creations in Christ, the old things having passed away, including the old ways of thinking (see 2 Corinthians 5:17). We are not to dwell on the things of this fallen world anymore. We are not to allow our mind to be mired in fear, doubt, frustration, anger, lack, depression, self-pity, anxiety, worry or anything else that does not line up with the truth that Jesus has done all and won all. He is seated in the place of honor and power. All authority in the heavenlies and on the earth is His. There is not one battle He has not won. There is not one victory He has not given us (see Psalm 24:8; Ephesians 1:20–22; 1 John 3:8).

Jesus has fully restored us to relationship with our heavenly Father and His Kingdom (see 2 Corinthians 5:18). He has given us the gift of His Holy Spirit (see John 14:16; Acts 2:38–39; 2 Corinthians 1:22). He has made us the overlap between heaven and earth (see Matthew 16:19). The more we allow our mind and our thoughts to be filled with these truths, the more we will manifest them in our lives. We are to set our sights on the realities of heaven. Heaven is real, and it is available to us here in the earth. It is the Kingdom that King Jesus has brought us into—not one day in the sweet by-and-by, but right here, right now. His instruction to us is to believe, receive and release the truth and reality of "on earth as it is in heaven" (see Matthew 6:10; 21:22).

There is no lack in heaven, no sickness or disease, no depression, no anxiety, no rejection, no fear, no darkness or defeat of any kind. That does not mean we will not encounter these things here in this fallen world; it means they are no longer our true portion, and we are not to dwell on them. We are instead to dwell on the realities of our new realm—heaven—a realm of righteousness, peace, joy, love, victory, provision, protection, light, an abundance of life, and every good thing. That is now our portion. That is our reality. That is our truth. That is what we are to focus on. We are not to ignore or deny the temporary facts we need to deal with here in the earth, but we are not to dwell on them. We are, of course, aware of the situations and challenges we face, but we fill our thoughts with the truth of who we really are and what we really have. Because when we do that, something far greater than our temporal challenges will be realized, revealed and released in our lives, and then into the world around us (see Romans 8:18).

Paul did not deny or ignore the fact that he was in prison. That was his temporary circumstance. But he chose not to dwell on the injustice or discomfort of it. Instead, he decided to focus on the good news of the Gospel, the great kindness of God and the faithfulness of his friends and co-laborers (see Colossians 1:6–8, 12–14). One of the ways we deal with our temporary facts is by focusing on eternal truth. This was the apostle Paul's secret to seeing even the most challenging and long-lasting "light and momentary affliction" become a gateway to a greater glory—a secret that he shared with the believers he mentored, and one we can grab hold of as well (see Romans 8:18; 2 Corinthians 4:17–18).

Think of Abram in Genesis 13. He was going through a challenging situation. His nephew Lot, whom Abram had brought with him, had been blessed due to their association. Instead of appreciating all he had come into thanks to his uncle Abram, Lot was actually crowding in on his uncle's territory. His herdsmen were arguing with Abram's herdsmen over land and grazing rights (see verses 6–7). Fights were breaking out. It was getting tense. In the natural, Abram had every right to take his nephew aside and read him the riot act. After all, everything Lot had was because of Abram. He had brought Lot with him. He had cared for Lot, fed Lot, looked after Lot, protected Lot, given Lot opportunities, put a tent over his head. And how had Lot repaid him? By trying to muscle in on his resources.

Despite the difficulty and injustice of the circumstances, Abram won the battle for his mind, and in doing so he saw a *light and momentary affliction* become his way into a *greater glory*. Abram fought off the temptation to let his thoughts go to a place of offense, anger, bitterness or frustration. Instead, he chose to dwell on the fact that no matter what was going on, he and Lot were family (see verse 8). He refused strife both in his mind and in his relationship with Lot, even in the midst of these disagreements. He then gave Lot his pick of the land, saying in effect, "You choose whatever looks best to you. I will trust my God and go find someplace else" (see verse 9).

Wow, what a champion. Think of a time when a member of your family treated you unfairly, spoke ill of you behind your back or just flat out did you wrong. It hurts when anyone does that, but with family it smacks even more. Family is supposed to be safe. Family is supposed to be there for you. Family is supposed to have your back. And yet instead of focusing on the hurt or the injustice, Abram chose to focus on the good—*we are family, no matter what*. Abram chose to love, favor and treat Lot like family, regardless of how Lot treated him.

Abram was operating in the Kingdom truth that dwelling on right thoughts is more important than dwelling on a specific plot of land. Abram chose to trust in the eternal goodness of God over the temporary challenges of his situation.

In doing so, he positioned himself for a greater blessing. It was not long after Abram refused to allow strife in his midst that the Lord spoke to him and blessed him with more and better land to the north, south, east and west, while also blessing his offspring and all his generations to come (see verses 14–17). The external blessing of multiplied territory, reach and influence happened because Abram was first willing to take the internal territory of his mind by stewarding his thoughts.

Our thoughts are powerful. They influence every aspect of our lives, including our emotional and physical realities. This is why the Word tells us in 2 Corinthians 10:5 to watch over our thoughts—to the point of taking them "captive" and making them "obedient" to the truth in Christ. The same Scripture says we need to cast down any thought that would try to exalt itself above the truth of God. In other words, we are not to allow our minds to be filled with negative, selfish, fearful thoughts, or any other thoughts that do not line up with the truth of God's Word. Instead, we are to focus on what is true, and honorable, and right, and pure, and lovely, and admirable—we are to think about things that are excellent and worthy of praise (see Philippians 4:8). Why? Because wrong thoughts—ones that catch us up in lies, negativity, ugliness, bitterness, anger, offense, selfishness, carnality and the like—have a negative impact on us.

Years ago, the Lord started mentoring me in this very thing. He tangibly manifested His presence in that moment and spoke very clearly to my heart, inviting me to "think about what I was thinking about, and feel what I was feeling." This was not an invitation to narcissistic navel-gazing and self-involvement; it was about operating as the dominion steward of my soul and becoming aware of the power of my mind. As the Holy Spirit helped me, I came to see how often my thoughts took me captive, as opposed to me taking them captive. He taught me how to monitor my thoughts so that when I noticed myself thinking things that were negative, self-destructive or out of alignment with the truth of God's Word and my born-again nature, I could "cast them down" and replace them with thoughts that were "obedient to Christ."

I am still learning to do this, but what I see again and again is that when I steward my mind—coming out of agreement with wrong thoughts and replacing them with Kingdom truths—it brings a powerful shift of atmospheres, first in me, and then eventually in my life. Winning the battle for our mind in the short term always sets us up for the spoils of those victories in the long term.

In the introduction, I shared a little bit about the decade-plus journey I have been on to overcome a variety of mysterious and at times quite limiting health challenges. About ten years ago, when the original symptoms were becoming more aggressive, I went to a series of doctors and had a litany of tests. This went on for about a year, and no one seemed to be able to get a handle on what was going on. I was getting weaker and weaker, sicker and sicker and more and more frustrated. A big part of my frustration came from not knowing what the issue was, and from having no clear plan of action or course of treatment. Some doctors even told me that it must all be in my head, because they could not find anything in my blood tests to indicate why I was so sick all the time.

Then one day, I went to see one of the doctors I was working with in the Phoenix Valley. He had recently ordered yet another slew of tests, and I was in his office that day to discuss the results. He brought out my folder and pulled out my latest lab results. After looking at them for a little bit, he announced that they showed I was dealing with an advanced case of Lyme disease. Those two words hit me like a gut punch. I knew about Lyme disease. I had lived in the mountains of Montana and had hiked the deer trails around my cabin almost every day for seven years, prior to moving down to the Phoenix Valley to be a part of starting the U.S. branch of our ministry.

The doctor was saying more words, but it was all just background noise to the thoughts racing through my head: *Lyme disease is incurable! Lyme disease is chronic! Advanced cases that have gone untreated can be aggressive and debilitating! Considering where I've lived and how long I lived there, why has no one ever thought to test me for this before, so it could have been caught earlier and dealt with sooner?*

I was afraid, frustrated and angry. And then, just as my thoughts were about to swallow me completely, the Lord broke in and very lovingly, but very firmly pointed out that I was focusing on the wrong thing. Instead of focusing on the name of Lyme disease and all its effects, He invited me to focus on His name and the fact that it was above every other name—including Lyme disease. In that moment, I knew I had a choice to make. I could continue to allow my mind to be filled with the fear and anxiety of my temporary facts: *I'd been diagnosed with a serious condition and was showing all the symptoms of an advanced case of this disease.* Or I could focus on the eternal truth: *My God is good, and in His goodness He has revealed what I've been dealing with for almost two years now.*

I could choose to fill my mind with fear and frustration, or I could choose to fill it with the truth that with God all things are possible, and that He is well able to heal what man says is incurable. My God heals leprosy. My God heals cancer. My God heals diabetes. My God heals lupus. My God heals plague. My God heals diseases of every kind, including Lyme disease.

I took a deep breath, and as I exhaled, I asked the doctor, "Can I have a minute?"

He got a concerned look on his face, but said, "Yes, of course. I know this is a lot to take in after all you've already been through."

I hopped down off his exam table and went over to the chair by his desk. I sat down, raised my hands up in the air and right there in the doctor's office, I began to praise the Lord out loud: "Thank You, Lord, that You have answered my prayers and have revealed what has been causing all these symptoms. You are good, and in Your goodness You have given me the name of what has been sent against me. I declare right here, right now, that the name of Lyme disease is not above Your name. But instead, it is Your name, the name of Jesus Christ, that is above every other name—including the name of Lyme disease. I command this thing to bow to Your authority, Your power and Your truth. By Your stripes I am healed. Lyme disease must go. Lyme disease must come out of my body. It must come out of every system, every organ, every gland, every muscle and every cell it has found its way into. It does not matter how long it has been there, because what You did for me two thousand years ago at the cross is greater and truer than any diagnosis or disease. Praise You, Lord!"

When I was done, I got up out of the chair, went back over to the exam table and said to the doctor, "Okay. What do you recommend we do in the natural while I continue taking care of business in the spirit?"

It was about a year later when that very same doctor gave me the news that my most recent round of tests showed that there was absolutely no evidence of even a residue of Lyme disease in my body. *Yay, God!*

I would love to tell you that this victory completely closed the door on any health challenges for me. But within a year, I was beset with another round of mysterious and progressively debilitating symptoms. The good news is, I had seen one victory in this area and knew I would see another, because in Him I already had the victory. Over the years I have not always walked things out perfectly, but the one thing I have learned (and that the Lord has graciously reminded me of again and again along the way) is that a key strategy to inhabiting my victory is to monitor my thoughts and cast down every one of them that tries to lead me astray into fear, self-pity, depression, anger, bitterness, offense or frustration.

I have had many opportunities over the ensuing years to grow in authority in this area through practice. I am so grateful to God for the revelation about the power of my thoughts, and for how He has faithfully mentored me along the way to win the battle for my mind. It is not that I never think wrong thoughts; it is that when I do, He is faithful to help me eventually take them captive, cast them down and replace them with the truth that I *am* healed by His stripes.

Today I walk in a great measure of the fullness of healing that has always been mine in Christ. I am able to travel, preach, minister and maintain a very full schedule. There are still some challenges, and they are real. But none of them is more real than the eternal truth of God's Word that I am healed by the stripes of Jesus (see Isaiah 53:5). That is the truth. That is what I set my mind on. And it is what I bring my thoughts back to when they try to wander off to anything else. Part of what helps me in this is that I do not even pretend to fully understand why it took years and years to see the manifestation of this truth. What I do understand is that God is good, His Word is true and I am a domin-ion steward of my soul. I would not wish what I have been through on anyone, but I also would not trade the reality of what I have learned in it all. I trust in the goodness of my God—the goodness of His promises and the goodness of His processes. He has helped me see in such a real way the power of my thoughts to create my reality and to affect the world around me. And because I got to choose all along the way that my God heals—period—I have been blessed to pray for many people in many places and have seen His healing power flow through me many times (even when I myself did not feel particularly strong). The truth that my God heals is established in my life because it is established in my mind.

Victor Not Victim

In His faithfulness, the Lord has even helped me change how I think about battles. When I find myself in a battle, I have learned not to waste time and energy by allowing my mind to be sidetracked with victim thoughts like, *Oh no, I'm being attacked!* Now, I think victorious thoughts like, *Yay, God, we're taking territory!* My 1996 New Living Translation of the Bible says in 1 Peter 5:8 that the devil "prowls around like a roaring lion, looking for some victim to devour." This is my favorite translation of this Scripture, because it makes it clear that it is *victims* the enemy devours. It is not that if the enemy attacks us, then we are victims. It is that he is seeking people who will take on the role of a victim when he attacks, so that he can then devour them.

The enemy can prowl around *like* a roaring lion, but he is not one. Christ, the victorious Lion of Judah, is the roaring lion! And because of Him, we are not victims; we are victors. Christ has given us the victory, and when the Lord blesses us with a battle, it is not because He has abandoned us or has allowed us to be outmatched. No. He blesses us with battles because we are made to co-labor with Him to take territory and advance the Kingdom in the earth. It is not the devil attacking us; we are attacking *him*, and the gates of hell shall not prevail (see Matthew 16:18–19).

The devil's only chance to devour a believer is if that believer stops believing, laying down the truth that we have the victory in Christ and taking up the lie that we are victims because the devil has attacked us. If we think of ourselves as victims, we become victims and give the devil opportunity to devour us. Not because he is so mighty, but because we have chosen to lay down our might by exchanging our overcomer's identity in Christ for a victim identity in our current circumstances. But if, instead, we choose to fill our mind with the truth that we are victorious in Christ, who has done all and won all, we will see that victory made manifest.

I do not make light of any temporary affliction you have been through or are going through right now. And I know even that word *temporary* can feel like an affront, because so often the affliction seems to go on and on. I have been there. I feel for you. But I also know how empowering it is to maintain an eternal perspective in the midst of even long-term "temporary" challenges. Let the Holy Spirit help you learn to identify the thoughts that try to sneak in and exalt themselves above the truth of God. Take those thoughts captive. Cast down those lies. I know they can look or feel true based on temporary facts, but if they do not line up with the eternal truth of who God is and all that He has given you, they are lies. Replace those wrong thoughts with the Word of God. Your mind is powerful. Do not surrender that power to the enemy.

Make Up Your Mind

Daniel is one of the great champions of the Old Testament. He was besieged, captured, trafficked, persecuted, attacked, thrown to the lions, mocked and more. Yet despite being victimized in a variety of ways, Daniel refused to be a victim. We see one of the keys to the way he did this in chapter 1, verse 8 of the book of Daniel: "Daniel made up his mind not to defile himself." It is right there: Daniel *made up his mind*. He made up his mind not to be defiled by the ways of the new culture that had been forced on him. He made up his mind not to partake of the things of that place and those people, because he knew they were not good for him. He made up his mind not to be a prisoner of bitterness and offense. He made up his mind to have power over himself, even if he did not have power over his circumstances. He made up his mind to have faith in God, no matter what.

The way Daniel chose to think about and respond to the situations he found himself in made all the difference in his life. Instead of being a victim, he was a victor. Instead of suffering all his days, he actually prospered and succeeded. He faced many challenges and difficulties, but by refusing to be defiled by the ways of the world he found himself in, and by always trusting in the goodness of God and the truth of His Word, Daniel saw the blessing, provision and protection of the Lord all his days. Daniel did not let his circumstances influence how he thought about God; he let how he thought about God influence his circumstances. Daniel *made up his mind*, and we need to as well.

Or as the apostle Peter put it in the New Testament, "Therefore gird up the loins of your mind, be sober" (1 Peter 1:13 NKJV). This makes it so clear. He tells us that we must gird up the "loins" of our mind. The loins are the region of our procreative power. The loins are what help bring forth life. By using this descriptive word, Peter is helping us see that as believers who are made in the image of the Creator, we have minds with creative power that we need to "gird" up. That word *gird* in the Greek is derived from *ana*, which means "each and every." He follows this instruction by telling us to be "sober," which in the Greek is the word *nepho* and can also be translated as "watch" or "abstain from." Or as the New Living Translation puts it, "exercise self control."

The apostle Peter is helping us see the importance of watching over every one of our thoughts, because our thoughts contain creative power. We must show self-control and bind wrong thoughts, negative thoughts, offended thoughts, bitter and angry thoughts, so that we abstain from giving them place and allowing them the power to create doubt, fear and darkness in us (and through us, out into the world around us). Peter wrote these instructions to the church in AD 63, near the end of his life. He had learned this lesson well. After all, as a much younger man following Jesus, he had been thrown for a loop when he did not understand what the Lord was doing in going to the cross. To Peter's natural mind, this was all a great defeat, and he let fear, doubt and confusion get the better of him—so much so that he ended up denying Jesus, turning from Him, abandoning his calling and going back to being a fisherman (see Luke 22:54–62; John 21:2–3). But an encounter with the Risen Lord helped Peter get his mind right and get back on track (see John 21:4–19). Peter learned that we must control our thoughts so that they do not control us.

Change Your Mind . . . Literally!

I hope you are catching the revelation of the power of your mind. In that process, however, you might also be realizing all the times you have let your mind be filled with wrong thoughts, negative thoughts and self-defeating thoughts. Or maybe it is dawning on you that when you have gone through challenging times, your response has too often been to murmur and complain, as opposed to finding something eternally true to focus on.

Here is the good news: That can all change today. It can change right now. Lamentations 3:22–23 promises that the Lord's mercies are there for you each and every day. He does not hold one wrong thought against you. He is thrilled that you are coming to understand the power of your mind. And He is right there with you, to help you start afresh. Think back to the story I told you about the photo shoot. As soon as I stopped allowing my mind to be filled with negative thoughts, and instead allowed it to be filled with positive ones, everything changed.

The same is true with the Lyme disease testimony. I chose to cast down fear, anger, frustration and other wrong thoughts, and instead, I filled my mind with the truth of God and His Word. That was the key to having power over the situation, as opposed to the situation having power over me. Then, over time, the truth that I knew I already had—that I was healed by His stripes—began to manifest increasingly as I chose to agree with it again and again, no matter what.

Learning to operate in greater and greater levels of dominion authority over your soul will allow you to operate in greater and greater levels of dominion authority in the earth. It is not that you earn more authority by doing it "right." It is that you are choosing to agree more and more with the authority you know you have in Christ.

If God is helping you see a pattern of wrong thoughts in your past, it is not because He is mad at you or disappointed in you. No. It is because He loves you and wants to help you inhabit more completely the fullness of what He has given you. He wants to help empower you to walk in a greater measure of the dominion authority that you have in Him. Or to put it really simply, He wants you to realize that when you change your mind, you change your reality.

Not only are God's mercies new for you each day, but in His mercy, He has created a way for you to grab hold of this "each day" newness specifically in regard to the power of your mind and how it affects your brain, body and reality. Our brains have some things called *neuroplasticity* and *neurogenesis*. Neuroplasticity is the ability of the brain to change and reorganize itself based on various stimuli or input. Neurogenesis is the creation of new neurons each day. This means that you can "change your mind" today by choosing to bring your thoughts into obedience with the truth in Christ. Cast down any "vain imaginations" based on temporary circumstances that would try to exalt themselves above that eternal truth of God (see 2 Corinthians 10:5). Then focus on things that are "pure" and "lovely" and "good" and "true." By doing this, you can actually change your brain and begin to program your new neurons with the new positive influences of these eternally true thoughts. Even if you have been doing it "wrong" for years and years—allowing your mind to be filled with bitterness, offense, anger, frustration and other negative thoughts—God has given you the ability to change your mind today and begin to shift everything to the good.

Deuteronomy 30:19 (NIV) says that "this day," God sets before you the choice of life or death, blessing or curse. He does not make us do what He wants. He is not a controlling God. He is a loving, empowering God who gives us a free will. He also gives us wise counsel and encourages us to choose to take full advantage of all He has given, done and made available to us. So even if you have made wrong choices in the past, know that today is a new day and a new opportunity to "change your mind" and start making choices—including the thoughts you choose to dwell on—that lead to life and blessing.

For instance, say you come from a family of smokers. Maybe your mother and father were addicted to cigarettes, and perhaps their parents were, too. So you grew up seeing this every single day, thinking it was normal. It was what adults did, so you figured that when you were of age, you would smoke, too. This may well have filled your conscious and unconscious mind every single day of your life. Of course you grew up to be a smoker.

But now, after years of being in the grip of this addiction, you see how damaging and self-destructive it is. The first step toward getting free is to change your mind. Stop thinking of smoking as normal, or as what adults do. Stop thinking of yourself as a smoker. Instead, change your mind. Start declaring today and every day that you are not a smoker. Tell yourself again and again. Say it out loud. Let the truth that you are free from this addiction fill your thoughts and your mind. Remind yourself that the Word of God says you have a choice, so you are no longer going to choose smoking and addiction and self-destruction. Instead, you are going to choose life and freedom and blessing. Let your mind be filled with this as your new reality.

As you make this change, remember the truth of Psalm 23:7—that as you think, so shall you be. Even if you find yourself reaching for a cigarette, declare again and again that you are not a smoker. Let that thought fill your mind even more than the smoke fills your lungs. Again and again. Day after day. There will be a change. That is the power of your mind.

Renew Your Mind

You can apply this not only to smoking; you can apply it to any addiction, or to anything that you have come into agreement with that is not God's very best for you. Perhaps you have parents and grandparents who have all suffered from diabetes or a certain type of cancer or some other sickness, and somewhere along the line you found yourself thinking, *Everyone in my family has had it, so I probably will, too.*

Those thoughts can actually affect you on a genetic level and increase the likelihood of that generational predisposition being triggered in you. But the good news is that positive thoughts, right thoughts, eternally true thoughts can actually have a positive effect on your genes. Thoughts like, *I am a new creation in Christ right down to my cells, genes and DNA. His blood has set me free from every addiction, sickness, disease and malady that my bloodline has ever suffered. Jesus has given me an abundance of life, the Holy Spirit quickens my mortal body and I will walk in the fullness of health, vigor, vitality and wisdom all my days.*

When we change our mind by choosing to come into agreement with the eternal truth of who we are and what we have

120

in Christ as born-again believers, our reality begins to change. The apostle Paul said it so well in Romans 12:2: "And do not be conformed to this world, but be transformed by the renewing of your mind." In the Greek, that word *renewing* can also be translated as "renovation." What Paul is letting us know is that a key to living in the fullness of Christ as believers is for us not to think like the world thinks, but to allow the Holy Spirit to help us overhaul our mind so we think about things from a Kingdom perspective.

What you come into agreement with has power over you. If you catch yourself thinking wrong thoughts or having a negative perspective on things, start declaring over yourself that your mind is being renewed. Ask the Holy Spirit to help you catch yourself in wrong thoughts so you can take them captive, cast them down and replace them with Kingdom thoughts.

Agreeing with eternal truth has real power. The challenge is that when we do not seem to see or feel that truth in our lives at a given moment, we can be tempted to think we do not have it. But that is how the world thinks: *I'll believe it when I see it.* We are not to be conformed to the world's way of thinking. In Christ we *know* we have it because His Word says we do. In the Kingdom we think, *I'll see it because I believe it.* We choose to think, dwell on and declare eternal truth over temporary circumstances. This has real impact.

I am the apostolic leader of Men on the Frontlines. As part of this ministry I am blessed to connect with, speak to, mentor and encourage men all around the world. We are very real with each other. One of the topics that often comes up, especially among the younger single guys, is how to deal with sexual desire and lust. The guys tell me that no matter how often they bind those thoughts and imaginations, they just never seem to go away. I understand. I was celibate for the first eleven years of my walk with the Lord (until He blessed me with my wonderful wife). This is a real issue, and it does no good to ignore it or sweep it under the rug. Guys think about this stuff. Telling them not to rarely works. Trying to push away wrong thoughts is not an effective strategy. It often empowers more wrong thoughts since you are actually dwelling on them as you try to push them away. (Remember that whatever you focus on, you empower.) So I share with the guys what the Lord helped me discover. Start with binding the bad, yes. But once you do that, quickly move on to loosing the good: *I am pure. I am holy. I am the very righteousness of God in Christ. All my needs are met by my Lord, who loves me.*

If we will dwell on eternal truth—declaring it and letting it fill our thoughts and our mind—it will become established in us. And if we have to do it over and over again throughout the day, that is not a bad thing. That is not a defeat. That is an amazing opportunity to establish the truth in greater and greater measures, again and again.

This works with all the wrong thoughts the enemy tries to tempt us with. After all, God did not try to push away darkness; He simply declared, "Let there be light!" Darkness goes when light is released. No argument. No pushback. No delay. It works the same with our thoughts. Instead of trying to push away wrong thoughts, fill your mind with righteous ones. Dwell on thoughts that are good, pure, noble, holy— just as the apostle Paul says in Philippians 4:8. As you do this, your mind will be renewed.

The Mind of Christ

I want to close this chapter with this thought: Not only is your mind powerful, but as a born-again believer, you have at your disposal the most powerful mind in the universe. First Corinthians 2:16 promises that you have been given the mind of Christ. Dwell on that.

Who is the most brilliant person you can think of? Stephen Hawking? Madame Curie? Nikola Tesla? Albert Einstein? Winston Churchill? Leonardo da Vinci? Sherlock Holmes? How cool would it be if you got to think with their mind for one day, or even one hour? Having the mind of Christ is way, way better. God is smarter than any of those people, and much more real than Sherlock Holmes. He is more creative, wiser, more innovative, more compassionate and a better strategist, planner and administrator than any one of them (or anyone else you can possibly think of). And that is the mind you have been given—the very mind of Christ. Plus, you have the Holy Bible and the Holy Spirit to mentor you in how to think as He thinks. Because you have His mind, there are always true, honorable, right, pure, lovely, good and excellent thoughts for you to think on.

BATTLE KEYS

Practical ways to apply the truths of this chapter in your life:

1. Take an hour and practice monitoring your thoughts. Set a timer on your phone. You do not have to sit still, but during this time commit to thinking about what you are thinking about as you go about your day. Capture any thoughts that do not line up with the truth of God's Word or your born-again nature. When you catch yourself thinking negative, doubting, angry, fearful, bitter, offended thoughts, cast them down and consciously

replace them with Kingdom thoughts. Meditate on Scripture that declares eternal truth, until it fills your mind. For instance, if something does not go the way you had hoped and you catch yourself thinking, *Nothing ever works out for me*, cast that thought down. Consciously come out of agreement with it. You could say, "That's not true. I repent of those thoughts!" Then bring your thoughts into obedience to Christ by declaring Kingdom truth. Say something like, "I am blessed and highly favored. Good things happen for me because God is good, and I will see the goodness of God today and every day. I am growing in favor with God and with man." After you declare it, let the Kingdom truth fill your mind by meditating on it over and over again.

2. Is there an area in your life where you feel that the enemy has been attacking you, and you now realize you have taken on a victim mentality? Is it your finances? Your health? A relationship? Let's shift that today. Declare this over the area: "I am not a victim; I am a victor. Christ has given me victory in every area, including in the area of my _____. I repent of letting my mind be filled with victim thoughts. I cast them down and today pick back up the victor's crown that Christ has placed on my head. I shift my thoughts from feeling sorry for myself. The enemy is not attacking me; I am attacking *him*. I am not losing ground; I am taking territory. I will persist in faith. In the power of Christ, I will persevere and overcome. I take back the territory of my mind, and I will also recover anything and everything that has been taken from me. In Jesus' name, I declare this Kingdom truth."

3. What are the five topics that are most on your mind? Maybe they have to do with battles you face, or perhaps they are areas you would like to grow in. Whatever they are, make a list of five scriptural decrees—one for each topic. Meditate on the decrees and declare them each morning. As you do this, remember that you are helping create new, positively influenced neurons in the process. You are using your mind to inform your brain, your body and your day.

For example, if the topics you want to focus on are health, provision, the return of a prodigal, Christian character and wisdom, you could make a list of decrees to meditate on and declare that look like this:

Health: "I am healed by His stripes. The Holy Spirit quickens my mortal body. No sickness or disease may come near me. Christ has given me an abundance of life, health, vigor and vitality."

(From Isaiah 53:5; Romans 8:11; Psalm 91:10; John 10:10)

Provision: "My God meets all my needs according to His riches in glory in Christ Jesus. I am blessed coming in and blessed going out. The blessings of God are chasing me down and overtaking me. He has opened the windows of heaven over my life, and I cannot contain the blessings He is pouring out on me. The Lord gives me an abundance of every good thing."

(From Philippians 4:19; Deuteronomy 28:6; Psalm 23:6; Malachi 3:10; Deuteronomy 28:11)

Return of a prodigal: "As for me and my house, we will serve the Lord. I believe on the Lord Jesus and am saved, as is all my household. The Lord will reveal Himself to all my line, including those who are not asking. He will be found by those who are not seeking."

(From Joshua 24:15; Acts 16:31; Romans 10:20)

Christian character: "I am patient and kind. I never give up. I never lose faith. I am always hopeful, and I endure through every circumstance. As a child of God, I am equipped for every good work. I put on a heart of compassion, kindness, humility, gentleness and patience. Every day I love others as I am loved and forgive others as I am forgiven."

(From 1 Corinthians 13:4; 7; 2 Timothy 3:17;
Colossians 3:12; John 13:34; Matthew 6:12)

Wisdom: "I have the mind of Christ. Because Christ dwells within me, I know godly wisdom and instruction in all things. The Father of glory has given me a spirit of wisdom and revelation. The wisdom that I walk in is from above. It is pure, full of peace, overflowing with mercy, unwavering and without hypocrisy."

(From 1 Corinthians 2:16; 1 Corinthians
1:30; Ephesians 1:17; James 3:17)

5

The Power of Your Will

I've chosen to live by Your counsel.

Psalm 119:173 MESSAGE

Right up front, I want to be very clear. There is one main thing I am hoping you will get from this chapter. I want you to realize that your choices have impact. They make a difference. Not only in your life, but throughout all of creation. Perhaps the single most influential tool you have at your disposal as God's dominion steward in the earth is the power of your will.

As a born-again believer, you are in possession of a worldwide ministry. And I am not just talking about through the Internet and social media. It is through the decisions you make. When you decide whether or not to live by the will and ways of God, you affect not only your life and the lives of those around you; you also affect the world as a whole. It is right there in Romans 5:18–19 (NLT):

Yes, Adam's one sin brings condemnation for everyone, but Christ's one act of righteousness brings a right relationship with God and new life for everyone. Because one person disobeyed God, many became sinners. But because one other person obeyed God, many will be made righteous.

Notice that it does not say that because Adam sinned, he alone was condemned. Or because Christ walked in righteousness, He alone enjoyed this new life. No. It says that because Adam disobeyed God, sin entered the world. And because Jesus obeyed God, His righteousness was made available to all. Adam was the first earthly son of God. Jesus was the Son of God who came as the Son of man on our behalf.

We see here that when a son of the Father—someone made in His image and placed in the earth as His representative and dominion steward—makes a decision, that choice has influence for good or bad well beyond that individual's own life. Your decisions matter. They have global impact. When you choose to walk in fellowship with the Father, trusting in His goodness and obeying His loving will and ways, you are blessed, *and* you also open the doorway of heaven into the earth through you, to bring His light into the world. On the other hand, if you choose to rebel and go your own way, ignoring or disdaining God's counsel, Word and wisdom, not only do you open yourself up to the consequences of sin, but you also darken the world through your sin.

Before we go any further, it is important that we discuss the Bible's use of the term *son*. When God speaks of "sons" in His Word, He is not leaving out women. Sometimes translators, in their desire to reveal the inclusiveness of God's heart, will translate *sons* as "sons and daughters" to make sure it is clear that women are included. I honor the intent of these translators, but gently remind us all that every promise and blessing of the Bible is already inclusive. There is no male or female in Christ Jesus (see Galatians 3:28). That does not mean there is no such thing as gender; that means there are no inequalities with God, no exceptions, no exclusions. Every bit of God is for every believer—male and female.

Consider this: We never feel the need to translate passages about the *Bride* of Christ as the *Bride and Groom* of Christ, because it is unnecessary (see Revelation 19:7; 21:9). Not one male believer is left out of the promises and blessings of being the Bride of Christ. Just as not one female believer is in any way excluded from all that it is to be God's son. Jesus was the firstborn of many (see Romans 8:29). Any and every female and male believer who says yes to Him as Lord and Savior is restored to the fullness of relationship with our heavenly Father. Just as we can all be His Bride, so too can we all be His sons. The reason this is so important is because Scripture comes right out and says that all of creation is eagerly and anxiously waiting in anticipation for the day that the *sons* of God will wake up to who we are and arise:

> For the anxious longing of the creation waits eagerly for the revealing of the sons of God . . . that the creation itself also will be set free from its slavery to corruption into the freedom of the glory of the children of God.
>
> Romans 8:19, 21

That word *sons* in Romans 8:19 is *huios* in the Greek. It is not about being a male offspring. It is about being one who is in the very likeness of the Father. A *huios* is more than just a child of God. A *child* of God is the word *teknon* in the New Testament Greek—delineating one who has been set free from sin and reborn into relationship with the Father, through Christ. But a *huios* is something more than a *teknon*; a *huios* is mature. A *huios* has grown into the very likeness of the Father.

In the Jewish culture of the apostle Paul's day, when he wrote this letter to the church in Rome, being born into a family made you a *teknon*. What made you a *huios* was adoption. Now remember, the Jewish concept of adoption is very different from the Western idea of adoption. In the West, adoption means a child who was born into one family is legally made a member of another family. But in Jewish culture, a father actually adopted his own child. This was not to make the child a member of the family. This was to mark that the *teknon* had now grown through the various stages of development, discipling and education within the family and culture to graduate to the level of being a *huios*—or a "mature son." What this meant was that the child was no longer merely a child, but was now a "mature one" who could be entrusted by the father to be his representative in all things.

When we are saved, we are *teknon* in the Kingdom—a "child of God." All of creation sees the impact this has on us. All of creation is aware that the curse has been broken off us and we are no longer under the shadow of death, but rather, we are now full of light and life. And all of creation eagerly anticipates us growing up into the realization of what we have with and in the Lord as His dominion stewards—able to operate under His authority to set creation free, as we have been set free (see Matthew 10:7–8; Luke 10:19; John 14:12; 20:22–23). For not only have we been liberated by Him; we are also liberators for Him. He loves all of creation, and we can release His love, light, life, freedom, healing, revival and restoration everywhere we go, to everyone we meet. This is true not because we are Messiah, but because we are in relationship with our heavenly Father through Messiah. And in this relationship, we choose to love Him and to know Him, and by His power that is at work in us, we choose to submit to Him—His will, His ways and His Word.

This is what a *huios* is in the Kingdom. Male and female mature ones of God who know, love and trust their Father. Ones who have grown to look, sound, act and love more and more like Him, because they have allowed the maturing process to take place within. These ones have chosen to truly die to their old carnal nature and come fully alive as "re-presentations" of their Father in the earth.

Hebrews 5:14 makes clear to us what it is to be a mature one in the Kingdom as a New Testament believer. My 1996 New Living Translation Bible is my favorite version of this eternal truth: "Those who are mature . . . have trained themselves to recognize the difference between right and wrong and then do what is right."

How glorious is that? One who is mature in the Kingdom is clearly revealed as someone who has gone through a process and come out recognizing the difference between right and wrong. Not one who chooses to lean on his or her own understanding for deciding what is right or wrong. No. One who knows the Father through the Son so well that despite any temporary circumstances, he or she is still willing to trust in the Father's goodness, and in His authority in all things at all times. One who recognizes, according to God's will, ways and Word, what is right and wrong, and then chooses to obey. That is a *huios*. That is a mature son. And that is one who has authority in the earth, because that is one who is under the authority of the Lord God Almighty. These are the mature ones—male and female—that all of creation is longing to see arise and shine. These are the ones who will set creation free.

You are a child of God. Are you willing to be a *huios*, as well? All it takes is one choice—the choice to do what God has revealed as "right" whenever you have a choice to make.

True Authority

We see a clear picture of this "maturity" in the gospel of Matthew, when the Roman officer approached Jesus to ask for help with his sick servant back home (see Matthew 8:5–13). Jesus responded to the officer's request by saying yes, of course, He would come and heal the servant. But the officer said he knew that Jesus could simply send forth the word from where they were, and the servant would be healed. The Roman officer was confident of this because he understood the power that came from being under authority: "For I also am a man under authority, with soldiers under me; and I say to this one, 'Go!' and he goes, and to another, 'Come!' and he comes, and to my slave, 'Do this!' and he does it" (Matthew 8:9).

Did you catch that? Not the power that comes from *having* authority, but the power that comes from being *under* authority—being submitted to a greater power. The Roman officer lived this way. He knew that when he gave one of his soldiers an order, the soldier would obey his authority because it was not just the officer giving the order; every one of his orders was backed up by all that he was submitted to. His authority came from being under the authority of the entire Roman army—the greatest army in the earth at that time. And the Roman army's authority came from being under the authority of the Roman Empire—the greatest world system in the earth at that time.

Yet the Roman officer sensed something even greater with Jesus. He sensed that Jesus was submitted to an even greater force and an even greater Kingdom. He had confidence in Jesus' healing power because he recognized that Jesus operated in great authority that came out of His willingness to submit to the greatest authority of all—the Father. This willingness marked Jesus' entire earthly ministry. It allowed Him, as a man, to walk in the fullness of authority in His relationship with His Father. He was not only filled with the Holy Spirit; He was also completely submitted to the leading of the Spirit. During His time in the earth, Jesus did nothing out of order, out of alignment or out of the will of God (see Luke 22:42; John 5:19). He was totally submitted to the authority of the Father.

We know that Jesus is the Son of God, that He *is* God and that He has all authority. But when He was in the earth, the Son of God came as the Son of man. He came on our behalf, to fulfill our part of the covenant, all the while also modeling to us how to walk in the fullness of relationship that He was bringing us back into—by submitting to the authority of our Father in heaven. No man has ever walked in greater power or authority in the earth than Jesus did, because as the Son of man, using the power of His will, He chose to completely, utterly and totally submit to the Father in all things at all times.

The Roman officer picked up on this, and Jesus was blown away that he caught this revelation. When the officer speaks this out, Jesus proclaims that He has never seen any of His own people understand it so well (see Matthew 8:10). After all, the reason Jesus came was because we had not submitted to the Father's authority, but instead had chosen to rebel. The word in the Greek for Jesus' reaction to the Roman officer is *thaumazo*, which implies a deep appreciation. The Lord wants us to walk in the fullness of all He has made available to us. He desires us to operate as His dominion stewards in the earth, His "re-presentations." One of the keys to doing this lies in the power of our will, and in our willingness to submit to the authority of the Father. It is not that when we choose to do right, we get a reward of more dominion authority. It is that when we, in our free will, choose to do right, we *are* operating in our dominion authority. Remember, the first realm you steward is yourself.

Perhaps the best example of this in the New Testament is Mary. In the gospel of Luke, we see the angel Gabriel come to young Mary with a message from the Lord (see Luke 1:26–38). He was inviting her to be part of birthing the greatest move of God in the history of the earth. Through her, the Messiah would come forth to fulfill every sovereign promise of the Lord and bring restoration and righteousness to the whole wide world. This was well beyond Mary's understanding. She had questions; she had concerns; she was confused; she was afraid (see Luke 1:29, 30, 34). How could this be? How would this work? What would people say? What would her fiancé, Joseph, think?

Ultimately, however, Mary chose to lean not on her own understanding, but instead, simply and obediently to trust in the goodness of God. Mary chose to say yes to the word of the Lord and be His vessel unto the ultimate revival and reformation. Amazing! This is a picture of a mature one. This is a picture of a *huios*. This is a clear example of how using the power of our will to choose to walk according to the ways and word of the Lord—no matter what—has impact well beyond our own lives.

This passage in Luke ends with Mary declaring herself submitted to the Lord and saying, "May it be done to me according to Your word" (Luke 1:38). Oh, what a powerful prayer! One we can all learn from. And one that reveals the power we have through our will to allow the fullness of heaven to work in us, and then to explode through us, out into the world. Mary chose to submit; she chose to obey the word of the Lord even when she did not fully understand. This made the way for visitation and habitation, all unto ultimately birthing the greatest move of God that has ever been seen in the earth.

Just as we are all the "Bride" and "sons," we are also all "Marys." We are all capable of birthing great moves of God in the earth through the power of our will—by choosing to come under the authority of God and His wisdom in all things.

The idea of submission can be a scary thing to some. Unfortunately, many have had bad experiences where authority figures were overly controlling, manipulative, or took advantage of their position. A parent. A boss. A teacher. A coach. Because of this, submitting can sometimes feel like giving up control, or even like an invitation to becoming a victim. But with God, it is different. First, He is never controlling or abusive. After all, He is the One who gave us our free will in the first place. God is always about empowering us as victors. He did all that He did for us so we would never have to be victims again—of sin, of death, of corruption, of anything. When we choose to submit to God, we are not giving up our control; we are actually learning to operate in it. The only real control we have is our ability to choose—what we say, what we do, what feelings and thoughts we allow. Every choice we make is a choice between life and death, blessing and curse (see Deuteronomy 30:19).

Choosing to submit to the Father is not surrendering to control; it is responding to an invitation to walk in Kingdom empowerment. When we choose to do what is right and submit to the will of our wise, loving, blessing, protecting, trustworthy Father, we are not giving up our control; we are operating in our authority as dominion stewards and shutting the door on the enemy in the earth. When we allow the Kingdom to advance in us by choosing to agree with eternal truth and by submitting to the Lord, it cannot help but advance the Kingdom in the earth. Remember, we are *sons* of God. Our choices have amazing and powerful repercussions well beyond our own lives. All of creation is longing for us to realize this.

Choose to Make a Difference

The Bible is full of examples of the massive impact we have as believers when we walk in relationship with the Lord and choose to use the power of our will to submit to Him in our lives. When we look at the choices of Daniel, Moses, Abraham and the early Church believers in Acts, they all illustrate just how much influence we can wield—everything from affecting the person right next to us, to influencing the course of world rulers and nations.

Daniel, for example, chose not to defile himself with the practices and culture of Babylon (see Daniel 1:8). No matter what, he chose to submit to the ways of the Lord. This was challenging and even dangerous at times, but ultimately, it led to Daniel having massive impact on an entire nation, including influencing the most powerful man in the world at the time, King Nebuchadnezzar. Through his interactions with Daniel, this king received a revelation that the Lord was God (see Daniel 2:47–48).

Daniel's peers—Shadrach, Meshach and Abednego—had been through many tests and trials, but they refused to see themselves as victims and always placed their trust in the Lord (see Daniel 1:1–3). Their submission to His word and ways cost them everything and even got them thrown into a fiery furnace (see Daniel 3:1–24). But ultimately, their choice to trust in and submit to God brought them through their trials and into a place of massive influence. They were made leaders of the land and were the reason an edict glorifying God went forth to all the nations surrounding Babylon (see Daniel 3:29–30).

Moses was another such example. He had to choose to submit to the Lord again and again, even when it looked as if God had not shown up and done what He promised. Moses went to Pharaoh, just as the Lord had asked. He spoke the exact words the Lord had told him to say, yet Pharaoh still did not let the Israelites go. Just the opposite, actually. He increased their labors and hardship (see Exodus 5:1–14). Things went from bad to worse. The people turned on Moses. Moses turned to the Lord. He asked God what the deal was (see Exodus 5:20–23). Why had God not come through? What the heck should he tell the people since nothing had seemed to go the way the Lord had said it would? God's answer to all of it was "I am the LORD" (see Exodus 6:2, 6, 8).

Moses had to decide if he would trust in the trustworthiness of the Lord and submit to His leading, or if he would trust in his temporary circumstances. He chose to submit. He chose to believe. He chose to lean not on his own understanding. He chose not to decide for himself what was right or wrong in this situation. Instead, he chose again and again to do what the Lord had said. Each time Moses went back to Pharaoh, it looked as if the word of the Lord were not true. Until! Because Moses chose to trust in the Lord and His word more than his own human understanding, not only was an entire nation set free, but the Israelites also were loaded down with spoils and plunder as they left Egypt.

In Genesis 12–22, pretty much every step of Abraham's walk with the Lord involved him choosing to trust in God's word, God's goodness and God's ability to bring about His promises in the midst of one challenging set of circumstances after another. What was the end result of Abraham choosing always to believe, even when he did not always understand? He was blessed richly, his descendants multiplied into countless millions, they were promised ultimate victory by the Lord and through Abraham all the nations of the earth were blessed (see Genesis 22:16–18). The Lord spells out the reason for all of this quite clearly: It was "all because you have obeyed Me" (Genesis 22:18 NLT).

And then there is the entire book of Acts. Every one of the disciples in the Upper Room that Pentecost Day had to get past questions, concerns, delays, disappointments and so much more to be there. But ultimately, they trusted in the word of the Lord and refused to focus on anything other than the promise of the Father (see Acts 1:4). Because they chose day after day to submit to the leading of the Risen Lord, they saw an explosion of the Kingdom come into the earth that empowered them to go out and change the world.

The choices we make as believers have massive reach and impact!

Lean Not on Your Own Understanding

God not only reveals in Scripture the influence we have through the power of our will; He also shares keys that will help us walk consistently in this power. Let's look at a few, starting with Proverbs 3:5–6: "Trust in the LORD with all your heart and do not lean on your own understanding. In all your ways acknowledge Him, and He will make your paths straight."

It all starts with us trusting in the Lord. Trusting in His goodness, His power, His faithfulness, His heart. Trusting that He is trustworthy. We say, "Well, yes, of course He is!" Yet how often have we wrestled with this very thing when He does not seem to do what we think He meant, when we think He should, in the way that makes the most sense to us? Moses wrestled with this. After that first unsuccessful trip to see Pharaoh, Moses actually asked God why He had even bothered to send him if He did not intend to do what He said He would (see Exodus 5:22–23). Abraham wrestled with this (see Genesis 16:1–6). How do you think Ishmael was birthed? Peter wrestled with this. He thought at one point that Jesus going to the cross was a mistake (see Matthew 16:22–23). Is it any wonder that you and I have wrestled occasionally with trusting God, as well?

But here is more of the good news of our God: He does not hold this against us. Instead, He helps us with it. In the very next phrase in Proverbs 3:5, the Lord reveals the secret to trusting Him at all times—by leaning not on our own understanding. Do you see it? The way we get over wrestling with not always understanding what God is doing is to let go of the need to understand. It is not that the Lord wants us to turn off our mind. He simply wants us to trust Him to bring about His promises, His way, according to His timing. Not because He is a control freak, but because He is really good at it.

We need to trust in the Word of the Lord, and also in the ways of the Lord. Otherwise, all too often, instead of choosing to believe and obey, we will choose to come up with our own way to bring about the Lord's promises. This is what happened with Abram and Sara. When the promised heir had not yet shown up according to a timeline that made sense to them, it was not the promise of the Lord that they began to doubt; it was the way of the Lord. So Abram and Sara came up with their own way to bring about the promise. Abram chose to go lie with Sara's handmaid, Hagar. And wow, did that decision ever have repercussions—ones we are still sorting out throughout the Middle East and the world today.

If we are willing to do what Proverbs 3:6 suggests and acknowledge God in all our ways—in other words, in every situation and circumstance we find ourselves in—He will make our paths straight. He will bring us into the fulfillment of all His promises, purposes and blessings in the best, most efficient way that does the greatest good for us and for all of creation. Part of the challenge is that His way does not always look and feel like the best and most efficient way to us. But that is exactly why we are to acknowledge Him, as opposed to acknowledging our ability to fully understand what is actually going on. At times, it can look and feel as if nothing is going on and nothing is happening, or even as if things are going in the wrong direction. These are the times when it is the most important that we acknowledge God and lean not on our own understanding. This is when it is critical that instead of choosing to get out ahead of God and come up with our own solutions, we choose to believe, choose to obey, choose to be a *huios* and operate in our dominion authority by stewarding ourselves and using the power of our will to agree with the Word and the ways of the Lord.

Give Audience to God

James 1:16–19 reveals another key that will help us in all of this:

Do not be deceived, my beloved brethren. Every good thing given and every perfect gift is from above, coming down from the Father of lights, with whom there is no variation or shifting shadow. . . .

This you know, my beloved brethren. But everyone must be quick to hear, slow to speak and slow to anger.

Here we are reminded that the way we keep from being deceived and using the power of our will to rebel is to remember that God loves us and is good. Everything He does is good. Everything He allows is ultimately for the good. His promises are good, and so are His processes. His will is good, and so are His ways. There is no variation or shifting in Him. He is always good and always worthy of being trusted—especially when it looks and feels as if nothing is happening.

Inherently, we know this. Our born-again spirit is connected with the Lord deep unto deep. Our spirit is always aware that He can be trusted in all things at all times. It is never swayed or influenced by how things look or feel in the moment (or how long they have looked or felt that way). Our born-again spirit does not get impatient or afraid or anxious. It never rebels. It knows there is good in the promises of God, and in the wise way that He brings about the manifestation of those promises in our lives.

Our soul, however, can be a different story. Our soul can doubt; our soul can get anxious; our soul can wonder what the heck is going on. It is in our soul that we decide whether or not to believe and to trust. That is why we must operate as dominion stewards of our soul to win the battle for our will—choosing to walk in the ways of the Lord, even when we do not fully understand. The key to this is right there in James 1:19: "Be quick to hear, slow to speak." That word *hear* in the Greek is *akouo* and means "to give audience." When we have

141

questions, concerns, doubts, fears and anxieties, this is not the time for us to be giving voice to those emotions by murmuring and complaining. This is the time for us to give audience to the Lord. We need to be quick to give place to His goodness, faithfulness and trustworthiness. If we do, it will help keep us from anger—not to mention fear, frustration, doubt and all those other negative emotions that can lead us astray.

The word James uses in the Greek that we translate as "anger" in this verse is *orge*, and it has a meaning well beyond simply being upset. It can also be translated as "desire, as a reaching forth of the mind." In other words, James is telling us that in challenging times, the key to not getting up in our own head and reaching for our own solutions is to get our mind quickly off what does not make sense to us and onto the Lord and His no-matter-what, unshifting, never-changing goodness, truth and trustworthiness. Or to put it another way, when we are not sure what God is doing, we need to remember what He is like.

Louder and Louder

There is one other key I want to look at before we move on. It is in Genesis 15, the chapter where Abram cries out to God for an heir. In verses 2–3, he says to the Lord that all that He has done for him is wonderful, but ultimately, none of it really means anything unless he has a son to pass it all on to. The Lord answers Abram by assuring him that yes, He will give him an heir (see verse 4). But prior to this, what the Lord says to Abram is critical: "I am thy shield, and thy exceeding great reward" (verse 1 KJV). This is one of the greatest blessings of the Old Testament, and one of the greatest truths for every believer to grab hold of.

We know, of course, that there is nothing God gives us that is more wonderful or amazing than the gift of a relationship with Him. He is our greatest blessing. In addition to that truth, there is something else here. When we see and understand it, it will help keep us from ever getting off track with the Lord as we look forward to the manifestations of His promises in our lives. When the Lord declares that He is Abram's "*exceeding great* reward," He is not repeating Himself or doubling down on adjectives to emphasize how awesome He is. That word *exceeding* in Hebrew is *m'od*, and one of its meanings is "louder and louder." The Lord knows that Abram is about to share the deepest desire of his heart. And prior even to telling Abram yes, He tells Abram how to get to that yes. Abram is old. Sara is barren. It is going to be a journey into the supernatural with the God of the impossible. That sounds exciting, but let's get real—journeys like that usually involve a few challenges. The Lord knows what Abram will go through on the way to his deepest desire being made manifest. He knows what Abram will face, what he will wrestle with, what he will have to deal with and overcome. He knows how confusing the journey will be at times. He knows how tempted Abram will be to doubt, to panic and to come up with his own solutions. He knows temporary circumstances can scream at us when we are trying to stay in faith: *It's never going to happen! You're a fool to believe! It's not working! You'll never get what you want like this! If it hasn't happened yet, it probably never will! You better come up with your own way to get what you want—fast!*

This is why the Lord knew how important it was for Abram—and for all of us as children of faith—to win the battle for our will along the way, so as not to give in to the lies of our temporary circumstances, doubt God, choose to rebel and come up with our own solutions. The secret is always to let the reality of who God is and what He is like be *louder and louder* than the report of our temporary circumstances, or even our natural understanding—to let His faithfulness, trustworthiness, goodness, power and reality drown out the volume of any fear or doubt or worry. Oh, if only Abram had grabbed hold of this truth, the problems it would have saved him! And not only him, but also Sara, their future generations and all of creation.

For us as New Testament believers, this should be easier than it was for Abram. After all, we have the cross to look to. We have the blood of Jesus. We need to focus on these powerful reminders of God's certain faithfulness and generosity. We need to allow them to fill us completely with the truth that our good God has given us everything. They should be our constant reminder that He was willing to do all so that we could have all. With this in mind, no temporary circumstance, no matter how challenging or seemingly long-lasting, should be able to convince us that God will not come through in whatever we are currently facing. The key is to let the truth that our good, loving, generous God was willing to give us the gift of His Son when we were yet sinners be *louder and louder* in our ears and in our hearts than anything else. Even if it looks or feels as if He is withholding something from us in the moment, we will know that is just not so (see Romans 8:32).

The other thing that the Lord declared to Abram in Genesis 15:1 is that "I am a shield to you." For a shield to be effective, it must be kept in front of a person, between him and the attacker. When we are journeying forward with God, taking territory from the enemy and coming into greater manifestations of all God's promises and blessings, it is key that we keep Him ever before us. We must allow the reality of who He is and what He is like to be louder, more real and more true than any lie of the enemy or temptation of our hearts to give in to fear or doubt. This will go a long way in helping us win the battle for our will.

The Enemy Knows

The enemy knows how powerful you are. Do you? The enemy often seems to understand the power of our will more fully than we do. He knows very well the authority we have in the earth as God's dominion stewards, and he is well aware of the impact the choices we make can have on all of creation. He knew if he could get Adam and Eve to rebel in the Garden, it would not just be the two of them who suffered, but that suffering would enter the earth. He has known since God pronounced judgment on him that the offspring of woman would crush his head (see Genesis 3:15), and he has come against mankind ever since. He realizes that anyone—male or female—who walks in relationship with our heavenly Father holds the keys to his demise. His only chance to overcome such people before they overcome him is to tempt them into using the power of their will to turn against God. He tried it with Jesus in the desert, but failed completely (see Luke 4:1–11).

The enemy knows that he is now defeated and on borrowed time. He no longer has authority in the earth. His only opportunity to have real impact in this realm is if he can once again sucker us into doubting God, giving in to fear and using the power of our will to rebel and go our own way. In other words, he is waiting for any and every opportunity to hijack our authority. We see an allusion to this in Luke 4, after the enemy's third attempt—and third failure—at tempting Jesus: "That completed the testing. The Devil retreated temporarily, *lying in wait for another opportunity*" (Luke 4:13 MESSAGE, emphasis added).

The enemy never had another opportunity to tempt Jesus when He was in the earth. That was his one shot, arranged by the Holy Spirit (see Luke 4:1). It was a divine setup so that the Son of man could win for us the battle of the soul that was lost in the Garden of Eden. This was the first of every territory we ceded to the devil that the Lord took back through His ministry in the earth and His victory on the cross. Jesus knew very well the power of the will. He used it to win this battle. The devil's "another opportunity" that he was waiting for did not arise during the life of Jesus on the earth; it comes in the life of every believer. It is right now, in your life. You are now the Body of Christ in the earth. You are now the Lord's dominion steward. You now have the authority in and with the Father to impact all of creation through your choices. The devil knows it. And he really, really hopes that you do not, so he can easily sucker you into being tempted by the temporary report of challenging circumstances. He hopes you will be suckered into believing that God is not coming through for you, so you consequently will choose to doubt, choose to be afraid, choose to give in to fear, choose to rebel and choose to go your own way.

In John 14:12, Jesus shares something with His disciples that is a profound revelation: "Truly, truly, I say to you, he who believes in Me, the works that I do, he will do also; and greater works than these he will do; because I go to the Father." Jesus is saying this, in fact, not just to those who were with Him in that moment, but to all believers throughout time who are willing to listen to Him and learn from Him as they walk together with Him. He is saying to every disciple that if we believe in Him, then we can do the works He modeled to us while He was in the earth. He came to restore us to relationship with our heavenly Father. While He was doing this, He was also showing us what that relationship can look like. He was modeling to us what it is to be a son, a *huios*, a dominion steward, a "re-presentation" of the Father in the earth, having impact on all of creation.

For more than two thousand years, Christians have gotten excited about John 14:12. And well we should. This Scripture means that if we believe in the Son and walk with the Father, then in the power of the Holy Spirit we can preach the Gospel, heal the sick, work miracles, raise the dead, go about doing good, cast out demons, bring hope to the hopeless, love the unlovable and more. But in the midst of all the understandable excitement over the promise of this Scripture, we must not lose sight of the "because" of it. Jesus clearly tells His disciples that all this is possible *because* He would go to be with the Father. *Because* He would choose to lay down His life. *Because* He would choose to obey, even when it was difficult. *Because* He would choose to use the power of His will to agree with the promise of the Father, and also with the process of the Father. Jesus modeled for us not only what it looks like to walk with the Father in fullness, but also how to do it.

Do you want to do the works Jesus did? And greater? Awesome. You are made for it. And He has made it all possible for you. It all begins by believing in Him, and then also by doing what He did—beginning with choosing to agree with the will and ways of the Father above all else, even when it means having to "lay down your life" and die to self, die to fear, die to doubt, die to anxiety, die to the lie that God is not showing up for you because He has not worked according to your understanding or timeline. This is the power of your will, and you can use it to have global impact through every decision you make to trust in the will and ways of the Lord, no matter what.

Never make the mistake of thinking your life is small or insignificant. People may not always recognize your importance. The world may not fully realize how powerful you are. But heaven does. And I hope that now, after reading this chapter, you realize it, too. Every decision you make has reach and impact. The power of your will affects all of creation, every day. Truly, you are mighty.

BATTLE KEYS

Practical ways to apply the truths of this chapter in your life:

1. Ask the Holy Spirit to search your heart and reveal any areas where you have refused to submit to the leading of the Father.

2. What in your past makes it challenging to trust God in these areas? Let the Holy Spirit not only reveal the issue, but also heal the root of it.

3. Put feet to your faith that a shift has occurred. Ask the Holy Spirit for a first step you can take to walk out being submitted to the Lord in each area. He wants to help. He wants to build trust with you. No matter how small or simple the first step is, commit to doing it as soon as possible.

4. Keep track of the Lord's trustworthiness. Start a journal and fill it with testimonies of the Lord's ultimate

faithfulness in any area where you have hesitated or struggled to submit to His will and follow His leading.

5. Let the reality of who God is and what He is like fill you afresh. Take time to meditate on His love, faithfulness, generosity, goodness and how trustworthy He has proven Himself in your life. Think about the cross and how He has already done all and given all to you.

6. Declare this each day: "Lord, I trust You. I don't always need to know what You are doing, because I know what You are like. You are faithful. You are trustworthy. You are wise. You are always good, and always right. Thank You for leading and guiding me all the days of my life. May Your will be done."

6

The Power of Your Emotions

A fool vents all his feelings, but a wise man holds them back.

Proverbs 29:11 NKJV

How are you feeling right now? Did you recently get some good news that has you feeling happy, excited and expectant? Or maybe you got up on the wrong side of the bed today and you are feeling a bit out of sorts? We tend to think that our emotions just happen, or that they are a product of our circumstances. But the truth is, emotions are an aspect of our soul. We actually have dominion authority over them, just as we do over our thoughts and choices.

When God created us in His image, He created us with emotions because He has emotions. We are meant to feel, and to feel deeply, just as God does. It was because of His deep love for us all—His deep love for *you*—that He sent His

Son. It was for joy that Jesus endured the cross—the deep joy He felt at the idea of being reunited with you.

God has a myriad of divine emotions. They are part of everything He does. When He created the heavens and the earth—shattering darkness, filling the void and bringing divine order to the chaos—His emotions were part of it all, literally. Genesis 1:3 tells us that He declared, "Let there be light." That word *light* in the Hebrew is *owr*, and one of its translations is "happiness." The darkness that was shattered is the word *choshek*, which also means "misery, sorrow" (see Genesis 1:2). So the Lord made the earth a place imbued with His happiness—a happiness that drives out misery and sorrow. He then put us in this place of happiness, with the mandate to steward His creation. Isaiah 60:1–3 makes it clear that one of the ways we do this, one of the ways we deal with darkness in the earth and even gross darkness among the people, is to "arise" and "shine." When we do that, people will be drawn to our "light," our *owr*, our happiness. Simply put, one of the easiest ways to advance the Kingdom in this fallen world is to win the battle for our emotions by choosing to walk in our born-again, godly nature and be happy. Which, after all, is our divinely created state.

Genesis 2:7 (KJV) tells us, "And the LORD God formed man of the dust of the ground, and breathed into his nostrils the breath of life; and man became a living soul." When God breathed life into us, when He filled us with an expression of His "I AM–ness," that is the moment when we became living beings. That word *living* in the Hebrew is *chay*, and one of its meanings is "merry." Our original God-made state is to be divinely happy, which makes sense considering that the Word says in His presence is "fullness of joy" (Psalm 16:11). And we are made for relationship with Him. We are made for His presence. We are made to exist in an atmosphere of heavenly joy while here in the earth. The question is, Will we choose to live this way? The first realm we steward is ourselves, and we need to decide if we will rule our emotions or if our emotions will rule us.

The reason this is so important is because emotions are so powerful. When God created us with emotions, He pronounced that part of our soul very good, just like all the rest of us He made in His image. Our divine emotions are very good, and very powerful. When we connect with them and choose to feel them, as opposed to allowing other feelings to hijack our moods, it helps connect us into the heart of God. And when the heart of God is brought into a situation, truly anything is possible. After all, it was the heart of God—His love—that sent His Son to manifest in the earth as a man and do the impossible—live a righteous life and pay the righteous price so that all could be saved.

Each day, we have an important decision to make. In every situation we encounter, we must make a choice. Will we actively steward the realm of our soul and live from the holy emotions always available to us in our born-again nature? Or will we allow ourselves to be overtaken by the negative emotions that stem from challenging circumstances we encounter in this fallen world? This is the battle for our emotions.

Jesus showed us the power of holy emotions in Luke 7:11–15, when He went to the village of Nain. As He approached the village, He saw a funeral procession. He discovered that the ceremony was for a boy who had died, the only son of a widow. When the Lord encountered this woman who had lost everything, Scripture tells us His "heart overflowed with compassion" and He told the widow, "Don't cry" (verses 13–14 NLT). Then He went over and raised the boy from the dead. That compassion Jesus felt—that caring, that concern, that love, opened the door for the miraculous. That is the power available to us when we connect with God's heart, which is always full of love, hope, care, compassion and life. It is greater than any sadness, any tears, any loss; it is greater even than death. Jesus could have chosen to let anger, sadness, discouragement, frustration or outrage fill His soul, but instead, He chose to feel compassion. He chose to connect with the loving, caring heart of the Father. And it overflowed out of Him, bringing heaven to earth.

I am not promising that every time you steward the power of your emotions and choose to live from your holy, "made in God's image," "very good" emotions, you will see a resurrection. But I do know that when you act as dominion steward over the feelings you allow to fill your soul, you help bring heaven to earth by operating in light, as opposed to giving in to darkness. Think of Peter in Acts 10. His heart was in a place where he felt it was wrong to go to the Gentiles (see verse 28). But through a repeated vision the Lord softened Peter's heart toward them, so that when the invitation came to go to a Roman officer's house, he accepted (see verses 9–23). The result was revival breaking out and the Holy Spirit moving powerfully on everyone who was there (see verses 44–46). All because Peter was willing to have a change of heart—because he was willing to feel for those people in that situation what the Lord felt for them. Peter, at the leading of the Lord, was willing to win the battle for his emotions.

The feelings we allow to fill our soul have real impact. They affect us both emotionally and physically. Just as science is proving that our thoughts can influence our health, it is also showing that our feelings can do the same. A quick

Internet search will give you lots of interesting reading from leading researchers and medical groups about the interplay between emotions and health. But for a much simpler proof of how your emotions can affect you, just look in the mirror. You will quickly see how your mood affects your face and your posture. When you are feeling good and positive, you are upright and smiling, with light shining in your eyes. If you have given over to a dark mood, you will see that you are quite literally downcast, with a bend to your spine and negative slants to your brow and the corners of your mouth. Your energy level suffers, your motivation suffers, *you* suffer from those dark emotions.

Our moods also affect the people and places around us. Remember, we are "gates" (see Matthew 16:19). Whatever we allow ourselves to focus on and be filled with will be released through us, out into the world. This, of course, includes our emotions. Did you catch that in Luke 7:11–15, it said Jesus' heart *overflowed* with compassion? He allowed the care, concern and love of heaven for the widow to fill His soul, and it flowed through Him out into the world, radically and miraculously transforming the situation. This is the power of your emotions. But be aware, just as they have the power to create atmospheres of love, light and life, they also have the power to create atmospheres of negativity, darkness and death. For example, if you allow fear, anger, bitterness and offense to fill your soul, it will overflow out of you through murmuring, complaining and maligning. Negative emotions create negative atmospheres, which then tend to draw more negative people who are all too willing to jump in and complain right along with you. This is what the enemy wants. He wants you to suffer. And he wants to hijack your authority in the earth in order to spread the suffering.

But the good news is—and there is always good news in the Kingdom—if you are willing to break from a pattern of negativity in your life by choosing to dwell on the positive instead of the negative, by choosing to praise instead of complain, by choosing to give thanks instead of feeling sorry for yourself, you can shift things. Not only shift your mood, but even actual situations.

Think of Paul and Silas in Acts 16:22–35. They were in an awful situation. They had been arrested, stripped and severely beaten. Then they were thrown into a dungeon prison and clamped into painful stocks. And for what? Preaching the Gospel and working miracles. But instead of focusing on the injustice and unfairness of it all; instead of being bitter or offended; instead of allowing anger at the city officials to overtake them, or anger at God for allowing it all to happen; they chose to focus on the positive. They knew the Lord. They were saved. They knew God loved them. They were moving in their callings. Yes, their situation was painful and difficult, but in that situation they chose to rule their feelings instead of allowing their feelings to rule them. They took control of their souls. They won the battle for their emotions. And right there in the prison, they chose not to murmur or complain. They chose not to feel sorry for themselves, not to be angry, and not to be afraid. Instead, they chose to praise and worship the Lord. They chose to celebrate the eternal goodness of God in the midst of their currently not-good circumstances. The result? Heaven invaded earth. The prison was shaken to its foundations. All the doors of the cells flew open, and the chains of every prisoner fell off. By winning the battle for their emotions and not giving in to dark and negative feelings, Paul and Silas not only saw themselves set free, but they affected everyone around them, including their jailer and his family, who all ended up giving their lives to the Lord. This is the power of your emotions.

We are all going to run into challenges at times. There are going to be difficult situations you encounter in this fallen world. The enemy wants to use them to put you in a prison of negative emotions—locking you up in fear, anger, bitterness, jealousy and the like. But it will only work if you allow it to. If you are willing to watch over your soul and refuse to give in to the draw of negative emotions—even in the midst of challenging circumstances—then the enemy cannot imprison you in a dungeon of dark feelings. Just the opposite. You will walk in freedom no matter what you face, and you will very likely help set others free, because they will want to know how it is that you can be peaceful, positive and praising in the midst of difficulties. That is an open door to sharing the *good news* of the Gospel.

The truth is, you are not going to be perfect at this. Everyone blows it from time to time. But you do not have to be perfect. Because the perfect One came on your behalf and resisted every temptation, overcame every trial and won every battle—including the battle for your emotions—so that in Him, you can choose to live in the victory that is always available to you. Even if you have just blown it.

As a matter of fact, realizing that you have given in to negative emotions is a huge step in the right direction. After that, all you need to do is choose to come out of agreement with them. It is as simple as asking the Holy Spirit to help you be aware of the feelings you are giving place to. This is not about narcissistic self-examination. It is about the dominion stewardship of your soul realm. Oppressive emotions always try to slither in during difficult seasons, challenging times and frustrating setbacks. Give no place to them. Do not let them trap you in a fowler's snare of negativity that keeps you from soaring in the heights of glory and goodness that are always available to you in Christ. Instead, do what Scripture instructs you to do—tear down each and every one of them (see 2 Corinthians 10:4–5).

Say, for example, that you catch yourself murmuring and complaining about not getting a promotion at work, and you realize that you have become bitter and bummed out because you do not feel as appreciated as you think you deserve to be. Becoming aware that you have allowed bitterness and sadness to fill your soul is a huge first step in winning the battle for your emotions. The next step is to choose to stop complaining and to come out of agreement with sadness and negativity. You may feel sad about not getting the promotion and feel negative about not feeling appreciated, but what I want you to realize is that you do not have to feel that way. Sadness is not your portion. Hopelessness is not your portion. Lack of favor is not your portion. In Christ, you are blessed and highly favored, you have hope and a glorious future and all things ultimately get turned to the good for you (see Deuteronomy 28:2–14; Jeremiah 29:11; Romans 8:28). This is who you really are. This is your true and eternal reality. Focus on that. Let that fill your soul. And then give God thanks and praise that this is what your truth really is, not what you recently experienced.

Isaiah 61:3 says we have a mantle of praise available to us at all times, and when we "put it on," it lifts off the spirit of heaviness. When you feel heavy or sad or bummed out, do not give in to those feelings. Do not just shrug and say, "Well, that's how I feel." No. You are choosing to feel that way. You are coming into agreement with those feelings. You are letting your feelings rule you, instead of ruling your feelings. And you do not have to. You can do something to shift it. Start to praise God—put on praise instead of putting on sadness. If you commit to this Bible truth and choose to praise the Lord, it will bring a shift. You will eventually feel the change, and you will see that you really do have authority over your feelings. Way to go, dominion steward! You are well on your way to winning the battle for your emotions.

Shifting the Atmosphere

This past summer, I did an extended ministry tour through the United Kingdom and Eastern Europe. It was a very fruitful time, when we saw God move in powerful ways on many people and many places. There were salvations. There were miracles. There were healings. It was awesome. But it was also challenging at times. I was away from home for almost a month. The schedule was very full, with early mornings, late nights and one plane, train and car ride after another. Near the end of the trip, I had a late-night flight from Sofia back to London, where I was scheduled to wrap up the tour. That day, I had done two different long meetings in two different cities that were quite a ways apart. I had preached, ministered and prayed for people for several hours at each event. There had been nearly a dozen meetings in the last five days. I was tired. It was late. And I was at the airport, knowing I would not be back in London until nearly one in the morning, and would not be at the hotel until well past two. I just wanted to get on the flight, get a bit of work done and maybe even catch a little sleep. To help keep costs down on the tour, this leg of the trip had been booked on a super-cheap intra-European airline. I knew it was going to be cut-rate, and I was fine with that. After all, it was just a three-hour flight.

I had never flown this carrier before, though, so I was not quite prepared for what I was getting myself into. When I checked in, I found out that my bags were going to cost me more than my ticket. *Okay*. And that the flight had been delayed. *All right*. With no certain time for when we would actually depart. *Got it*. I made the best of the situation—found a place to get something to eat, had a cup of coffee, caught up on emails and messages, got some work done, finished a book I had been reading and then walked the airport to get some exercise. What I really wanted to do was to sit down and fall asleep, but I was concerned that if I did, I would miss the announcement about when our flight was ready to go.

Eventually, the announcement came. We had a departure gate and a departure time. *Yay!* I got in the long line (that seemed to move almost impossibly slow) and eventually had my ticket and passport rechecked, and I was cleared to board the plane. I walked through the gate, down the stairs and into another waiting area, where we were told they were having trouble with the buses that carry passengers out to the planes. The waiting area quickly filled up, and pretty soon we were standing shoulder to shoulder, one big mass of people. I am tall, so I at least had the advantage of having my head up above the crush of the crowd. I looked around and saw a sea of tired, frustrated, downcast travelers. I put a small smile on my face and looked a few people in the eye. My smile was not returned. I tried the same thing with some of the airline workers. Same result. The atmosphere was heavy, almost oppressive.

Eventually, a bus came. The first group of passengers was loaded on for the trip out to our flight. After a while, the bus returned. It was my turn to board. It was standing room only, and I guess they did not think the bus had more than one last trip in it, so they tried to pack all the rest of us on. They crammed us in there like sardines. Once they had packed everyone on, the doors of the bus closed. We started forward. And then almost immediately stalled and stopped. The driver got out and disappeared. Maybe it was time for his break? A little bit later he got back in the driver's seat and started the bus back up. We drove about ten feet, and then the bus stalled and stopped again, lurching us all forward rather dramatically. Once again the driver got out and disappeared.

About this time, a family who was pressed up against me started to have a bit of a meltdown. The boy all of a sudden became very, very upset and threw a fairly massive fit. The parents tried to deal with it by out-yelling him, but then, when they realized that was not working, they just gave up while he cycled up and pretty much went nuclear.

I am a fairly introverted person when I am not preaching, and I tend to like quiet and order. This situation would have been a stretch for me even when I was well rested and prayed up, let alone when I was exhausted and already pretty much near my natural limit of patience. Bottom line . . . I did not handle it well. Oh, I did not blow up or yell or do anything like that. What I mean is that I pretty much totally failed at watching over my soul and being a dominion steward of my feelings. I think I started with muttering, "You've got to be kidding me?" And then I went into full-on frustration, with a dash of offense, all while allowing self-pity to run rampant and thinking to myself, *This is the worst airline ever.*

At that moment, the Holy Spirit initiated a gloriously convicting conversation: *When I called you to ministry, what did you say?*

Yes, Lord.

When I shared with you that ministry is releasing the Kingdom into the earth through your life, what did you say?

Yes, Lord.

When I called you to be a traveling itinerant, what did you say?

Yes, Lord.

When I asked if you would be willing to go to challenging places and bring breakthrough in challenging situations, what did you say?

Yes, Lord.

What about here? What about now?

I would love to tell you that I immediately responded, *Yes, Lord.* But the truth is, I wrestled. My flesh felt as though this was all a bit much after all I had already poured out over the last several weeks. Oh, how selfish and ugly our old carnal nature can be. But the Holy Spirit always knows just what to say to help get me past myself. And this moment was no different: *Feel thankful. At least it is not a night and a day in the deep, like Paul.*

So true. At that moment I realized how silly I was being. And how selfish. I love being an itinerant minister. I love releasing the Kingdom into the earth through my life. I love preaching, praying and prophesying regions open, bringing breakthrough to people and places. Why not here? Why not now? I took a deep breath and quietly repented, "Thank You, Lord, for the blessing of going for the Gospel. Please forgive me for my wrong attitude." I then pivoted around toward the family I had quite literally turned my back on. I caught the eye of the mother and asked, with compassion in my voice and care in my eyes, "Long day?"

She looked at me for a minute, and I smiled. Then she said, "You have no idea."

Her husband joined the conversation and told me that they had been on holiday for two weeks and that their trip home had started early that morning on a train that also had all sorts of problems. It had been one delay after another, one problem after another all day long, and all they wanted to do was get on the plane, get settled in and get home.

I told them I was so sorry for all they had been through. They apologized for their son's meltdown, explaining how he had actually held up quite well through most of the day's challenges. At the mention of his name, the boy turned to give me a once-over, lip still quivering, seemingly undecided about whether he would go back for another round of screaming or not.

While he was looking at me, I asked him, "What was the best part of your holiday?"

He stared at me. To be honest, I was not sure if he was considering my question or considering whether he had enough room in the packed bus to pull his leg back and kick my shin. But after another moment he replied, "The ants."

I asked what he meant, and he told me all about an anthill he had found and how fascinating it was to watch the ants building and working together. His mother chimed in that he loved bugs. I told him I knew very little about bugs and always thought they were a bit icky, but I would love to hear more. So he began to share all the wonderful things about bugs. He was thrilled to have an audience and had completely forgotten about throwing a fit.

His mother caught my eye and silently mouthed, "Thank you."

At that moment, I heard the bus start back up. I turned and saw the driver had returned. It seemed that the bus had been fixed, and we were on our way to the plane. The mood in the airport, the waiting area and the bus had been heavy. I had allowed it to affect me instead of me affecting it. But thanks to the Holy Spirit helping me see this, I was able to make a shift first in myself and then in the atmosphere, which ultimately helped shift the entire situation.

We got to the airplane. I had a new appreciation for bugs, as well as having a new little buddy. I found my seat, settled in, and because I had been able to catch up on all my work while waiting for the delayed flight, I was able to put my earbuds in, listen to some worship music and sleep most of the way to Heathrow. *Yay, God!*

Buying into Emotions

One of the biggest challenges in winning the battle for your emotions is coming to understand that just because a situation stirs a feeling in you, that does not mean you have to give place to that feeling. Too often, we approach our emotions with the attitude of, *Well, that's just the way I feel.* But we have a choice. We have control.

Think of it like this: When you go to the grocery store, there are all sorts of different foods to choose from. Shelves and aisles are packed with choices: boxes, cans, fresh food, frozen food. It is all there. It is all real. It is all available to you. But you do not have to put all the food in your cart and leave the store with it. You have a choice. You can choose something you know is good for you, like broccoli or an apple or some oatmeal. Or instead, you can load your cart up with Twinkies, even though you know they are not a very good choice. But you do not have to put Twinkies in your cart. Or, if you already have them in your cart, it only takes a moment to realize they are not good for you and decide to take them out of your cart and put them back on the shelf. You do not have to leave the store with the Twinkies. You do not have to take the Twinkies home. But even if you do take the Twinkies home, you do not have to open them. Or in the middle of opening a pack of Twinkies, you could still decide, *Wait, these things are terrible for me. I'm not going to eat them!* You can even decide after one bite that a Twinkie is not a good choice, and you can throw the rest of it away. It is never too late to make a quality decision about the food you put in your body.

It works the same with the emotions you allow in your soul. At any given moment, you might feel angry or frustrated or afraid. And it would be real. In that initial moment you would be feeling that feeling, but you do not have to give over to it. You do not have to give place to it. You do not have to take it off the shelf of possible responses, load it into your cart, pay for it at the register, leave the store with it, take it home, unwrap it and eat the whole thing. At any point in the process of choosing to give place to that emotion, you can stop and make a quality choice not to buy into it. You are the steward of your soul. You can win the battle for your emotions.

With that in mind, let's talk about a few of the most common negative emotions. The better understanding you have of them, the easier it will be for you to identify them when they are still "on the shelf," so you can choose to leave them there, as opposed to putting them in your emotional cart and taking them home with you.

Fear

Dun-dun-duuun. You can almost hear the foreboding horror movie music that even the word *fear* chimes in our souls.

Fear was a direct result of the Fall. After eating the forbidden fruit, Adam hid from God because he was afraid (see Genesis 3:10). When we feel fear, it is a good indication that we, too, are "hiding" from God. Hiding some part of our *self* or some part of our life—keeping it from Him—often without even fully realizing it. Way down deep, we are aware that we are out there on our own in this area, and fear creeps in. Fear of missing out. Fear of being exposed. Fear of not having enough. Fear of rejection. Fear of losing something (or someone). Fear of being harmed. Fear of failing. Fear of not measuring up. Fear of being disappointed. Fear of making a mistake.

Fear of any kind is an indication that we have removed ourselves from God in some way. I do not mean removed ourselves as in denying He is Lord and losing our salvation. What I am getting at is that when we feel fear, it is a clue that we are not abiding in the Lord, trusting in Him as our source, our worth, our approval, our protection, our provision, our truth, our path, our wisdom, our *all* in that situation or set of circumstances.

Fear is basically the granddaddy of all negative emotions. So much so that when I find myself wrestling with negative feelings, one of the first questions I ask the Holy Spirit is to help me see what it is I am afraid of. I might be feeling anger or frustration or anxiety or impatience, but at the root of it is a fear issue—something I am not trusting God with or trusting Him about. It never fails. It is always ultimately a fear issue. The great thing about turning to the Holy Spirit and simply asking Him for help in understanding what it is I am afraid of is that the very act of asking, in itself, helps defeat the fear—because asking Him the question brings me back into His presence. God is the great antidote to fear. He is perfect love, and according to 1 John 4:18, "Perfect love casts out fear."

Think of Jairus in Mark 5. He was a big-deal synagogue official. He had position. He had title. He had influence. He had standing in the community. He had prestige. He had wealth. He basically had all that the world had to offer in his day. But he put it all on the line for one simple reason—his daughter was sick unto death. Jairus had heard about the miracles Jesus supposedly was performing. He knew going to Jesus for help could cost him everything, since as a synagogue leader he was supposed to be in line with the high priest and take a stand against Jesus, not be seeking Him out for help. But Jairus did not care. He loved his daughter more than he loved his position. He loved his daughter more than he feared losing everything. So when Jesus was in town, Jairus went and fell at His feet and pleaded with the Lord to come to his home and heal his precious daughter (see verses 21–23). Jesus, of course, said yes.

Jairus must have been thrilled. He had risked everything, but it had been worth it. The Miracle Worker was coming to his home. His daughter would be healed! But as they began the journey to Jairus's house, a crowd gathered. It became a throng, and it began to slow them down (see verse 24). And then a woman appeared. She, too, was desperate for a healing. She grabbed hold of Jesus to pull on His healing virtue and got her miracle (see verses 25–29). She also brought the entire procession to a halt. Jesus was so moved by her faith that He stopped to talk with her (see verses 30–34). By the time this encounter was wrapping up and Jesus was once again about to start on His way to Jairus's home, messengers arrived to tell Jairus that his daughter had died and that there was no use bringing Jesus to the house (verse 35).

Put yourself in Jairus's shoes. He had put everything on the line for his daughter, and it had worked. Jesus was on His way to his house. But then . . . that woman! She pushed her way in and slowed everything down. She got in the way. She stole his daughter's miracle! Imagine the emotions Jairus must have been wrestling with. Anger. Frustration. Jealousy. Sorrow. Discouragement. Grief. Disappointment. Bitterness. Self-pity. Despair.

Yet how does Jesus deal with it all? He says to Jairus, "Do not be afraid any longer, only believe" (verse 36). Jesus goes right to the root—*fear*. Every emotion surging through Jairus was ultimately sourced in fear, and Jesus presented him the choice we are all presented with when we wrestle with negative emotions: *Are you going to give in to fear and all the feelings it is causing to swirl inside your soul, or are you going to believe in Me and the truth that no matter how overwhelming things seem right now, I am bigger and more able than your current circumstances?*

Jairus had a decision to make: Would he continue to fear, or would he allow Jesus to help him believe? He chose to believe. He chose to continue walking with Jesus. The whole way home, Jairus must have had to win the battle for his emotions over and over again, continually pushing away fear and choosing faith. This was possible because he had chosen to walk with Love Himself. Step by step. Decision by decision. Jairus chose to trust in God, as opposed to giving in to fear. The end result was that he saw the Lord do something even greater than healing his daughter; he saw the Lord resurrect his daughter.

When we turn to the Lord to help us conquer fear, it opens the door to something even greater than what we were initially believing for.

Anger

Scripture tells us not to sin with our anger, for it can give the devil a foothold in our lives (see Ephesians 4:26–27). And yet we also see in Scripture that there are times when God was angry. How can this be, since God never sins? He never gives place to the enemy or to darkness of any kind (see 1 John 1:5). It is because there is a significant difference between the anger of man that stems from our old selfish, carnal nature, and the righteous anger of God (see James 1:20).

God's righteous anger is against sin because sin separates us from Him, and the Lord adores us above all else. His anger is not against the sinner. God loves the sinner (see Romans 5:8). So much so that He sent the gift of His Son to pay the price for all sin for all time, so that all could have eternal life and be restored to the fullness of blessing in relationship with Him (see John 3:16). Simply put, the Lord loves us utterly, but there are times when He does not love what we do (sin). This does not cause Him to withdraw His love from us. His anger at sin does not make Him angry at us. Yet He does not want us to sin. He hates sin, because it brings harm to our lives (and then through our lives, to the people and places around us).

Righteous anger does not withdraw love or break relationship. Righteous anger does not punish the person for his or her poor choices or wrong actions. Righteous anger is against the devil and his works. This is not the anger that we wrestle with. This is not the anger that we need to watch out for in the battle for our emotions. The anger of man is not a righteous anger; it is a selfish anger. It is an anger that is not for others, but against others. It is an anger that wants to lash out, punish, hurt or retaliate when we have been hurt. It is an anger that comes from fear and frustration and offense. It is an anger that serves self, not the Kingdom in the earth.

A clear example of this is in Luke 9, when Jesus and the disciples were walking to Jerusalem. Jesus planned for them to stop in a Samaritan village along the way. He sent a few of the disciples ahead to prepare for His arrival (see verse 52). But the Samaritans were offended that Jesus was going on to Jerusalem, so they refused to receive Him (see verse 53).

When James and John heard about this, they got angry, so much so that they said to Jesus, "Lord, do You want us to command fire to come down from heaven and consume them?" (verse 54).

Jesus responded by warning them to be careful because they did not realize what their hearts were like. He reminded them that the Son of man did not come to destroy men, but to save them (see verses 55–56). Jesus was mentoring His disciples in the difference between man's anger and God's. Jesus was not angry at the Samaritans. He was not angry that they did not receive Him. He was not angry that He and the disciples were not going to get a break and the chance to get some water and maybe a meal from the Samaritans. He knew the Samaritans were not His source. He knew that no matter what things looked or felt like in the moment, He would ultimately always have everything He needed and would be taken care of completely by His Father in heaven.

Jesus knew that He and the disciples were not going to the Samaritan village for themselves, but for the Samaritans. The only thing Jesus felt, I believe, was compassion for the Samaritans. Jesus wanted to share Himself with them, but the Samaritans had lost the battle for their emotions by choosing to come into agreement with a spirit of offense. In that, they also lost an opportunity for a visitation of the Lord. This, I believe, is what grieved Him—not that He and His disciples were turned away, but that offense had closed the door on Him being able to spend time with the Samaritans.

James and John, however, were mad. But it was not a righteous anger. They were not mad about what the enemy and his spirit of offense had stolen from the Samaritans. They were mad at the Samaritans. They wanted to punish them. They wanted to see them burned up. They wanted to see those nasty old Samaritans pay for not receiving them. James and John's anger was selfish; it was carnal. James and John had lost the battle for their emotions. But Jesus was there to work with them. He did not hold their anger against them. He did not withdraw from them or punish them. He continued to walk with them (see verse 56). He continued to mentor them, so much so that John was transformed from a "Son of Thunder" into the apostle of love (see Mark 3:17).

It is the same with you. When the Lord helps you see an anger issue in your life, it is not because He is angry with you. It is because He loves you and wants to help set you free, so that you never give place to the ravages of the enemy in your life through unrighteous anger ever again.

Disappointment

The danger of disappointment is right there in the word itself. When we give in to this negative emotion, it actually works to "dis-appoint" us. God has appointed us as His dominion stewards in the earth. We are to rule and reign in His authority, on His behalf, all to His glory. We advance the Kingdom by knowing, being in relationship with and trusting the King— trusting in who He is, trusting in what He is like, trusting in what He has done, trusting in His Word and trusting in

His ability to bring about what He has promised. When we give in to disappointment, it is a sign that we are no longer trusting God. We are no longer in faith. Disappointment is a red flag signaling that our hope is no longer in God and His Word above all else. When we give in to disappointment, what we are actually doing is declaring that God has failed to meet our expectations according to what we think should have happened, how it should have happened and when it should have happened.

We might be disappointed in a person. We might be disappointed in a situation. We might even be disappointed in ourselves. But ultimately—if we are a people of faith who trust God with our relationships, circumstances and lives—when we choose to give place to disappointment, we are choosing to believe that we understand how to bring about the promises of God better than He does. Our authority as expressions of the Kingdom in the earth comes from being under His authority. Disappointment takes us out of that place of being under the authority of God, because we have decided we know better than He does.

We are going to encounter challenges in this fallen world. As a matter of fact, in John 16:33 Jesus even promises this. But He also promises that there is no need to despair in these challenges, because He has overcome the world. In John's first epistle, he helps mentor us in how to step into this victory even in the midst of challenging circumstances. He tells us it is through our faith in Christ (see 1 John 5:4). In other words, sure, we are going to have situations we do not understand and may even not like, but as long as our hope is in Christ, we ultimately never really will be disappointed.

One of the greatest antidotes to the poison of disappointment is the cross. We become disappointed because we feel as though we have been hit with a setback or defeat. A job does not come through. A door does not open. People do not do what they promised. A blessing we think for sure is going to happen does not come our way. A breakthrough we are expecting looks and feels delayed. The latest medical report still has bad news in it. And so on. These are real situations, but we need to realize that what looks and feels like a defeat or "disappointment" in the natural, very often in the Kingdom is actually a divine setup for breakthrough, promotion, acceleration and advancement.

Think of the cross. To all the world, the cross looked like a great defeat. It was not. The cross was so not a failure. The cross was so not a setback. The cross was the greatest and most significant victory of all time. Yet even Jesus' disciples failed to see it for what it was. Why? Because they were leaning on their own understanding. They were all so convinced that they knew how Jesus was going to restore the Kingdom in the earth that they completely missed the victory of the cross. They knew the promise, but they had stopped trusting in the Promiser—even though He had clearly told them what He was going to do and how it was going to go (see Matthew 16:21).

God has clearly told you what He is going to do. He is going to prosper you. He is going to bless you. He is going to heal you. He is going to provide for you, protect you and restore you. He is going to increase you. And more. We know the promises (see Exodus 23:25; Deuteronomy 7:13; 28:2–12; Psalm 91:3–8; Isaiah 53:5; Jeremiah 29:11; Philippians 4:19; 1 Peter 5:10). To avoid being disappointed, it is even more important that we know and trust in the Promiser. That we trust in how He chooses to bring things about. That we trust in His timing. That we trust in His wisdom, His will and

His ways above our own understanding or feelings. This is the key to avoiding the trap of disappointment.

Several years ago, when I was in the midst of my journey to overcome a series of serious health challenges, the Lord had to mentor me in this very thing. I had just arrived back in Eastern Europe. I was doing some preaching and ministry when my strength allowed, but the main reason I had returned was for another round of medical care and therapies that were unavailable to me in the United States. I had gone through two months of treatments and returned home for a month, and now I was back for another three months of daily trips to the doctors, hospitals and labs. I was not doing especially well at this point, either physically or emotionally. I had been believing and fighting in faith for years, yet was sicker and weaker than ever. I was a withered shadow of my former self and was often so weak and shaky that I could barely stand for any length of time.

Whenever I went to minister, the anointing of God would come upon me so strongly that I could preach for an hour and pray for people and work miracles after that. But as soon as the tangible anointing lifted, I would end up in bed for days at a time. My first night back, I was having trouble sleeping due to the jet lag from a nine-hour time difference. I was sitting in the living room of the apartment where I was staying, pouring my heart out to God. At one point I asked Him, "Lord, what is Your strategy for me during this trip? Is there anything I need to do that I haven't already done?"

He immediately spoke to my heart, answering that the focus of this trip was for me to learn how to delight in Him, no matter what. His presence was tangible.

My heart soared, and I said, "Yes, Lord!" After all, when you are in His manifest presence, it is easy to delight in

Him because He is delightful—quite literally full of delight since there is fullness of joy in His presence (see Psalm 16:11). The visitation with Him lasted for quite some time. I ended up falling asleep on the couch in the living room and getting the best few hours of sleep I had had in quite some time.

The next day, I had appointments with the main specialist I was working with, and I also went to the lab for blood draws, scans and other tests this specialist had ordered to get a current read on how I was doing. The news was not good. This began several weeks of dire test results and discouraging responses to the treatments, therapies and injections I was receiving. After the first month, I was wrestling with disappointment, discouragement and fear.

On another night when sleep seemed as if it just would not come, I was back on the couch in the living room, pouring my heart out to God. I was reminding Him of all of His promises about healing me. I was reminding Him about all the unfulfilled promises and words over my life. I was reminding Him about how long the battle had gone on, and how long I had been standing on those promises. And I let Him know I was really, really tired. I did not know what else to pray. I did not know what else to decree. I did not know what else to declare. None of it seemed to be working. I could clearly see His promises in the Word, but that almost made it harder—knowing they were right there in front of me, knowing they were true, but also knowing they just did not seem to be for me.

My heart was breaking, and at one point, with my voice also breaking, I cried out to the Lord, "Just what exactly am I supposed to do?!"

He immediately responded, *I told you. Delight in Me.*

I asked Him if He had been paying attention the last few weeks—there really was not much of anything to delight in.

His response was a very tender reminder that He had not instructed me to delight in my circumstances; He had invited me to delight in Him. He then went on to share how proud He was of me for having learned to stand on His promises over and over again throughout the years of the battle. He told me that, yes, knowing His promises, believing His promises and standing on His promises was important and powerful, but in the times when it looks and feels as though the promises are not coming to pass, it is more important and powerful to focus on the Promiser than the promises. That was the way to avoid giving in to disappointment in a long battle.

He then took me to the book of Numbers, where He told Moses to send twelve spies into the Promised Land (see Numbers 13:2). When they got there, all twelve of the spies clearly saw the promises of God right in front of them. It was a magnificently fruitful land flowing with milk and honey, abundant in every good thing, just as the Lord had said (see Numbers 13:21–24). But when they returned to Moses and the people to give their report, ten of the spies shared that yes, they had clearly seen the promises of God, but they would never be able to have those promises because the enemy in the land was so big and so strong and so well established (see Numbers 13:27–29, 31, 33). Sure, they could see the promises, but they just could not see how the promises would ever be theirs. Their report was so disappointing that the people ended up being greatly discouraged, and they began to turn against God (see Numbers 13:32–33; 14:1–4).

There were two other spies, however, Caleb and Joshua, who had a different report. They told the people that the land was amazing, and that sure, there were some enemy strongholds here and there. But since the Lord had said He would give them the land, they should all trust in Him and go take it (see Numbers 13:30). They told the people to get over themselves and stop being so negative. They pretty much told them to get control of their souls, win the battle for their emotions and trust in the Lord (see Numbers 14:6–10).

The difference between the two reports? All the spies clearly saw the promises of God, but the first group of spies was so focused on the strength of the enemy and the difficulty of the situation that they felt the promises would never be theirs. Caleb and Joshua were focused on the Lord. They trusted in Him and His strength more than anything else. They focused on the Promiser and His faithfulness even more than they focused on His promises. They delighted in the Lord. This kept them from the place of disappointment. This helped them win the battle for their emotions. And it will help you and me, as well.

I realized that night that I was behaving like the Israelites in Numbers 13 and 14. I was listening to the discouraging report of my circumstances and giving in to disappointment. Yes, my situation was disappointing. Yes, the recent test results were disappointing. But those were simply facts. Facts change. God does not (see Malachi 3:6). And that is the wisdom of focusing on God and delighting in Him in the midst of challenges, disappointments and long battles. When we choose to delight in the Lord no matter what, it shifts our focus from temporary facts to the eternal I AM. It shifts our attention from things that are disappointing to the One who never is.

Disappointment is hope deferred, and it can make the heart sick (see Proverbs 13:12). If we put our hope in how things look or feel at any given moment, we will be like the wrong group of spies. But if we choose to be like Caleb and Joshua and put our hope in the Lord, the Promiser—even above hoping in His promises—our hope can never be deferred, because the Lord never fails (see Deuteronomy 31:8).

Offense

One of the first things my mentor ever told me when I started out in ministry was to watch out for offense, because it would take me out of my calling more quickly than almost anything. The reason for this is because offense is all about the *self*. We take offense when we do not like what is being said, or we do not like what is being done, or we do not like how we are being treated. When we take offense, we are making it all about ourselves, and that is a trap. Offense mires us in *self*, which means we are no longer abiding in Christ—the place of victory, protection, anointing, provision, favor, blessing, strength and more. The trap of offense is that we think we are defending ourselves, protecting ourselves and standing up for ourselves, but what we are really doing is stepping outside the one truly safe place—Christ.

This is how Jesus put it: "For whoever wishes to save his life will lose it; but whoever loses his life for My sake will find it" (Matthew 16:25). The word *life* there is the Greek *psuche*, and one of its translations is "the rational soul." So we could loosely translate what Jesus is telling His disciples here this way: If you want to fight for what makes sense to your feelings, you are going to end up losing everything Jesus came to give you. But if you are willing to get past what feels right or fair to you in the moment and trust in Him, ultimately you will find everything you desire and were created for, because the only place any of us can truly find those things is in Him, the Messiah.

In other words, choosing to take offense is one of the quickest ways to lose the battle for your emotions. Offense is the *self* trying to save itself, protect itself, set up boundaries for itself. That never works. In the moment, it may feel as if it works, but ultimately, what offense does is cause us to turn away from another person. In doing that, we are also turning away from Jesus and the Kingdom. We are not called to take offense when someone does us wrong; we are called to love that person (see Matthew 5:44). We are not called to turn away from someone who speaks ill of us; we are called to bless and pray for that person (see Luke 6:27–28). We are not called to go off in a huff when someone sins against us; we are called to forgive and show that person a grace he or she did not show us (see Matthew 6:12; Romans 12:14). We are not called to fight against someone who has come against us; we are called to fight *for* him or her (see Ephesians 6:12).

In the Kingdom, when someone does us wrong, we are not called to self-protection; we are called to die to self and double down on love. We can do none of this when we take offense, because offense causes us to pull back and wall off from the very person God may be trying to reach through us. Think of it like this: Offense is "a fence." It is an emotional boundary we create between ourselves and someone else because we do not like how that person behaved. But is that what Jesus modeled to us? No. Is that what He meant when He said we will do the works that He did and greater? No. Jesus never took offense. Jesus never turned away. Jesus never withdrew love, even when He was treated horribly.

If we want to walk in the fullness of the Kingdom here on earth, we need to do what Jesus has called us to and what He modeled for us—love, no matter what. Sure it might sting at first, but ultimately, it will work to witness the reality of the glory of the goodness of the Gospel to that other person, and it will help us to come even more fully alive as the new creations we are in Christ. Death comes before resurrection. Dying to self and refusing offense is a fast track to walking in greater manifestations of His resurrection power (see Philippians 3:10–11).

In John 6 we see very clearly how offense causes us to separate from Jesus. In this passage, Jesus is teaching about how He came down out of heaven to bring eternal life to the world, and about how important it was to take part of the fullness of who He is through the communion meal of His body and blood (see verses 47–59). But the people are not getting it. They are having a hard time seeing past the fact that this is Joseph and Mary's son (see verse 42). They are struggling with what He is saying and teaching, and they are thinking, *How can He be from heaven? What is He talking about with all this "eat My body and drink My blood" stuff?*

Even Jesus' disciples are wrestling with what He is saying. So much so that Jesus asks them directly, "Does this offend you?" (verse 61 NLT). Many of the disciples could not get past it. They turned away from Jesus and abandoned Him (see verse 66). This is what offense does. It not only causes us to shut off our hearts to another, but ultimately, it causes us to "abandon" Jesus—to abandon the One who is Love.

You may be thinking, *Wait just a minute! I would never abandon Jesus. I would never turn my back on Him.* But that is what happens with the trap of offense. It causes us to turn from our born-again nature that is Christ within us. When we choose to take offense, we are choosing to let our heart harden. Based on another person's behavior, we are choosing to withdraw love. This is not what Jesus did. This is not what Jesus modeled to us. And this is not what Jesus called us to. When we choose to take offense, we—just like those disciples in John 6—are choosing in that set of circumstances to abandon Jesus.

There is one more thing we need to talk about in regard to offense. Offense is *taken*. It is a choice. Just because an offense is given does not mean you need to pick it up and run with it. We live in a fallen world. We are going to encounter broken and hurting people—in and out of the Church. And yes, at times they will do offensive things. But just because someone does something offensive to you does not mean you need to take offense. You have control. You have the ability to choose whether or not you take offense. People did offensive things to Jesus all the time, but He never took offense. And in Him, we have the ability to walk in that victory as well. In Him, we have the power to win the battle for our emotions and refuse to take offense, no matter how we are treated.

Self-Pity

When I was a new Christian, a friend of mine gave me a teaching by Joyce Meyer. One of the things she said in it has always stuck with me: "You can be pitiful, or you can be powerful, but you can't be both." That perfectly sums up the danger of self-pity. It makes us pitiful, not powerful. Self-pity is more than just feeling sorry for yourself; it is coming into agreement with the lie that you are a victim, not a victor. Self-pity disempowers us. Self-pity causes us to surrender our place as dominion stewards in the earth who can positively impact our circumstances and surroundings. Self-pity makes us defeated complainers who lie down for the enemy.

Think of the Israelites in Exodus 14. God had done everything He said He would. He set them all free from the bondage of Egypt, and He brought them out loaded down with the spoils of the land (see Exodus 12:31–32, 36). He provided for them and cared for them every step of the way (see Exodus 13:16–18). And now He was setting up Pharaoh and his armies for complete, utter and total defeat (see Exodus 14:4, 28). But as the soldiers and chariots of Pharaoh approached, the Israelites began to murmur and complain, and to feel sorry for themselves (see Exodus 14:11). They gave themselves over to self-pity and took on a total victim mindset. So much so that they began declaring that they would prefer to be back in bondage in Egypt (see Exodus 14:12). That is the danger of self-pity. It causes you to choose a victim mindset that disempowers you and ultimately returns you to bondage.

Moses was facing the exact same situation as the rest of Israel, but instead of choosing self-pity, he chose to turn to the Lord. He cried out to God. He refused to feel sorry for himself. He refused to murmur and complain. He refused to give up. This put Moses in a position for God to remind him what he had at his disposal. The Lord told him to stretch out his staff and speak to the situation (see Exodus 14:15–16). When he obeyed, the Lord opened up a path through the Red Sea. All Israel went to the other side, unscathed. And the enemy was totally wiped out. Moses refused self-pity. Moses refused to be a victim. Moses refused to be pitiful. So instead, he was able to be powerful and see the Lord use him mightily to impact his circumstances and deliver a nation.

The thing about self-pity is that it feels like such a justified and even rational response to difficult circumstances. That is what makes it so seductive and dangerous. But now you know the warning signs of self-pity—feeling sorry for yourself, murmuring, complaining, telling everyone what a tough time you have had and how unfair it all is, focusing more on the attack of the enemy than the goodness of God, carping about what the Lord has not done more than celebrating what He has done. Now you will be able to catch it in its early stages and not give place to it. When you feel self-pity trying to get hold of you, remember that in Christ you are powerful, not pitiful. Use that power to win the battle for your emotions by refusing to come into agreement with self-pity.

Remember Who You Really Are

God created us to feel, and to feel deeply. But He also created us with the ability to rule our emotions so that they do not rule us. You are a dominion steward in the earth, and that includes being a dominion steward of your feelings. When you are feeling angry or afraid or offended or depressed, do not simply accept those feelings as your lot. Take control of your soul. Win the battle for your emotions.

You may not be able to shift instantly into feeling something positive, but you can shift your focus, and ultimately that is the key. Get your eyes off the problem, the person or the "impossible" situation, and get your eyes onto God. Choose to give your focus to Him, His Word, His truth, His character and nature. Praise Him. Worship Him. Let the reality of who He is, what He has done and what He is like fill you afresh. Let His perfect love cast out all fear. Let Him who is Peace overwhelm your anxiety. Let His joy bring light to any darkness that is trying to grip you.

Remember what God is like, and remember that you are made in His image. Let Him remind you of who you really are, and then let every negative emotion that does not line up with that fall away.

BATTLE KEYS

Practical ways to apply the truths of this chapter in your life:

1. Practice connecting with the heart of God and learning how to feel what He feels. Ask the Holy Spirit to bring a person to mind. Then ask Him how He feels about that person. If you wrestle with negative feelings toward that person, ask the Holy Spirit to help you put those feelings aside so that you connect with God's heart for the person. Let His divine feelings fill your soul. Allow yourself to feel what God feels—the love, the joy, the good pleasure—until your heart overflows with those feelings. Pray and intercede for the person from this place of God's abundant heart. This also works really well when you are in the middle of a disagreement with a spouse, family member, co-worker or friend. Taking the time to let your heart be filled with God's feelings, and praying from a heart that overflows with love for that person, can cause a "resurrection" in a damaged or "dead" relationship.

2. Think of a difficult, disappointing, frustrating, infuriating or discouraging situation you feel trapped in that has you locked up in negative emotions. Now bring the Lord into the situation by praising and worshiping Him right while you are in the midst of it. Maybe it is a health situation. Maybe it is a difficult marriage. Maybe it is a lack of finances. Or maybe it is a prodigal who just

seems to get further and further away from the Lord. Be like Paul and Silas. Take a moment in the midst of what you are going through and refuse to be afraid, bitter, offended or negative in any way. Instead, praise God. Worship Him and give Him thanks. Sing His praises, no matter what is going on around you. Do this every day, until the "chains" break off and the "prison doors" spring open. And be sure to watch for the early signs of the victory—the triumph of your being free of the negative emotions in the midst of the difficult situation. If you are not sure how to start, simply commit to saying with passion, "Praise the Lord, O my soul, and all that is within me! Praise the Lord! Praise the Lord! Praise the Lord!" Commit to doing this ten times in the morning when you first get up, and then again at night before you go to bed. (Scriptural decrees you make in faith are powerful. The more you decree them, the more you establish the eternal truth of God's Word in your life.)

3. Move in the opposite spirit of a negative emotion by declaring the truth of a positive one. When you catch yourself feeling irritable and impatient, declare who you really are by decreeing the scriptural truth that "I am patient and kind!" (see 1 Corinthians 13:4; Galatians 5:22–23). Do the same with any negative emotion that tries to come upon you. Cast it down by declaring the truth of the divine emotion that your born-again spirit is filled with. By doing this, you are being a dominion steward of your soul and causing it to come into agreement with your born-again spirit.

4. The next time you find yourself in a heavy or oppressive atmosphere, practice arising and shining. Refuse to

be influenced by the negativity, and instead, influence the negativity by partnering with the Holy Spirit to release the light of heaven into the darkness through your emotions. Perhaps it is with a heartfelt smile or a kind word, or by responding with peace and patience to a person who is wrestling with irritability. Commit every day to positively influencing an atmosphere through the overflow of divine emotions from your heart. This will teach you not only to steward your emotions, but also how you can influence atmospheres around you through your emotions.

7

The Power of Your Words

For out of the abundance of the heart his mouth speaks.

Luke 6:45 NKJV

If you want to get a good idea of how you are doing in winning the battle for your mind, will and emotions, pay attention to the words you are speaking. Our words pretty clearly reflect and reveal what is going on in the depths of our soul. It says so right there in Luke 6:45—our words come forth from the heart. That word *heart* is *kardia* in the Greek, and it can be translated as "the physical heart," but also as our "thoughts and feelings." We tend to give expression to what is going on in our heart and mind. It can be with a look on our face. It can be with the posture of our body. But very often, it is our words that are the clearest indication of what is going on in our souls.

Think of God—for He so *loved* the world that His Word manifested in the earth to save us all (see John 1:14; 3:16).

187

From the very depths of God's heart, He sent forth His Word. While we, of course, are not God, we are made in His image, and similarly, our words come forth from within us and have an effect on our world. Our words are formed and informed by our thoughts and emotions. They are powerful. And they do create.

Genesis 1:1–25 and Hebrews 11:3 make it clear that God spoke all the world into existence. Over and over again, "God said" and something came forth (see Genesis 1:3, 6, 9, 11, 14, 20, 24, 26, 29). He created creation by sending forth words. He then made us in His image and placed us in creation as His dominion stewards (see Genesis 1:1–28). One of the ways we steward creation is through the words we speak. It is very revealing that the first job God gave to Adam as His steward in the earth was to speak forth the names of all the animals (see Genesis 2:19–20). From the very beginning, God was mentoring us in how to use our words to inform creation. Our words frame our reality.

Want a clear picture of the impact of your words? Think of the last time you said something positive, affirming, loving and supportive to your spouse, your child or a friend. You probably saw an immediate effect from declaring someone's worth and value. The person might have smiled, stood up a little taller or gotten a twinkle in his or her eyes. Contrast that with a time when you lost your temper and yelled at someone, spoke out of frustration or said something harsh. The person probably turned away, slumped or flashed anger back at you.

It works the same with the words you speak over yourself and your circumstances. Your words have power, both in the natural and in the spirit. We are little creators made in the image of the Creator. God created with His words. And so do we. When we win the battle for our mind, will and emotions, we choose to speak words out of our soul that are in agreement with our born-again spirit. These are words that exhort, edify and encourage. These are words that release light, not darkness; life, not death; blessing, not curses. When we choose to speak such words, they have real impact in the earth. They tear down the things of darkness and establish the things of the Kingdom.

Think of the prophet Jeremiah, to whom God revealed the impact of words. The Lord appointed him to stand up against powers and principalities in the earth. The way He equipped Jeremiah to do this was by putting His words in Jeremiah's mouth. God let Jeremiah know that he had the power to destroy strongholds and build up the Kingdom—all simply through the words he chose to speak (see Jeremiah 1:9–10).

You may be thinking, *Yeah, but that was Jeremiah. He was a great prophet.* But remember, Jesus Himself said that the greatest prophet—even greater than Jeremiah—was John the Baptist, and that the least in the Kingdom is greater than he (see Matthew 11:11; Luke 7:28). That means that *you*—even if you think you are the least in the Kingdom and have barely squeaked in by the amazing grace and mercy of Jesus—can greatly affect creation through the words you speak. Your words have power. God knows it. And you need to know it, as well.

No Coarse Thing

In Ephesians 4:29, we are warned not to let any corrupt, foul, coarse or abusive language come forth from our mouth, but instead to let everything we say be good and helpful. This is not because God is a delicate flower who cannot handle some rough language. It is because He knows our words have power. He knows our words create. He knows our words can work for us or against us.

In Luke 1, we read about the priest Zacharias. He was an old man, and his elderly wife, Elizabeth, was barren. But they very much wanted a child. One day Zacharias was serving in the Temple, burning incense before the altar of the Lord. The angel Gabriel appeared to him and told him that the Lord had heard his prayers and was going to give him and Elizabeth a son. The angel went on to speak many amazing things about the boy—that he would bring great joy and gladness to his parents; that many would rejoice at his birth; that he would be great in the eyes of the Lord; that he would be filled with the Holy Spirit even before he was born; that he would cause many to turn to the Lord; that he would have the anointing of Elijah; that he would precede the coming of the Lord; that he would change disobedient minds to accept godly wisdom and that he was to be named John (see Luke 1:11–17). A remarkable list of promises. And yet, when Zacharias heard all this, the first things out of his mouth were words of doubt and negativity (see Luke 1:18). He did not give thanks. He did not praise the Lord. He did not speak in agreement with any of the promises. He gave voice to fear and disbelief.

Gabriel struck him mute—not because he was mad at Zacharias, but because he understood the power of Zacharias's words better than Zacharias did. The other thing Gabriel did immediately was to make a positive statement in agreement with the promises, declaring that the word of the Lord would come forth. Gabriel shows us some important Kingdom truths here. First of all, it is better to say nothing than to murmur, complain or say something negative. Second, if we do make a negative statement, it is important that we come out of agreement with it and counteract it by releasing words that are positive and are in agreement with the truth of God.

When we speak words of fear, doubt and negativity, they have impact. They can work to hinder, delay and interfere with our promises. Gabriel would not let anything work against the promise of the Lord. When he struck Zacharias mute, he was helping Zacharias get out of his own way, until he could come to understand the power of his words—which Zacharias did. Months later, shortly after John was born, all the friends and family were saying that the boy should be named Zacharias after his father. But Zacharias used his words to write down a definitive statement agreeing with the word of the Lord that the boy's name would be John.

Instantly upon doing that, Zacharias was able to speak again (see Luke 1:61–64). He had come to realize the power of his words, and the power of speaking in agreement with the word of the Lord. The first words out of his mouth this time were praises unto God. Zacharias had won the battle for his mind, will and emotions. He had taken control of his soul and come out of agreement with doubt and disbelief. Now he was stewarding the promises of God in his life through words of agreement, praise and thanksgiving, as opposed to hindering the promises through words of negativity and fear.

Your Words Have Impact

In Isaiah 55:11, God reveals that when He sends forth His word, it accomplishes what it is sent to do. It is the same with your words. They have impact. They accomplish what they are sent to do. That is why it is so important that you watch over your words. God wants to fill your mouth with His words—words that bubble up out of your born-again spirit; words that shine light and love and life; words that go forth to lift up, cheer up and build up the people and places you encounter; words that are in agreement with His promises and eternal truth. But the enemy wants to hijack the authority of your words and use them to release death and darkness. He wants to mire you in pessimism and bitterness, so that you speak forth words laced with anger, fear and frustration—words that hurt, words that tear down, words that spread doubt and negativity.

The Israelites murmured and complained their way through the desert. Is it any wonder that what should have been about a two-week journey ended up taking forty years? When you speak against the promises of God—when you give voice to fear and doubt and discouragement and disappointment—it works against you and delays the promises of God in your life. But if you are willing to win the battle for your mind, will and emotions and choose to speak words of faith, hope and encouragement—even in the midst of challenges, tests and trials—it will work to establish and accelerate the things of God in your life, and in the earth.

In Job 22:28, it says that we can "decree a thing, and it will be established." When you speak words of faith that are in agreement with the promises of God, those words work to bring the promises forth and make them manifest. But be aware, words of fear and doubt work the same way. They are negative decrees, and they will work to push away, delay or deny the promises of God. Words of fear and doubt are like muck released from your mouth, which will slow you down and get in the way of advancing into the promises of the Lord. Words of faith and hope are like a thick, rich oil that smooths your path and quickens your journey. It is critical that you come to understand the power of your words.

Life and death are in the power of your tongue (see Proverbs 18:21). When you speak life-affirming, life-uplifting, life-agreeing words, you are filling and imbuing your life with the *zoe*-life of God (*zoe* means the Spirit-quickened, abundant liveliness of divine life). But if you choose to speak negative, mean, angry, fearful, bitter, coarse, foul words, you are actually sowing death into your life—death of hope, death of faith, death of joy, death of promises made manifest. But fear not. Even if you have at times spoken wrong words, Jesus never did. He completely won the battle for the mind, will and emotions—including the battle for the power of your words. Jesus was the very Word of God made flesh. He was always in agreement with the Word of God, because He was the perfect expression of God's Word. You are in Him, so you are in His victory. Simply repent for any wrong words you have spoken, and ask for His help in speaking only life, faith and truth from now on. The blood works not only to forgive you, but also to redeem and renew you—including your words.

When I was going through the different stages of the battle for my health, there were many difficult and discouraging days. I have already shared different aspects of that journey with you, but one of the most important things the Lord taught me—especially when the battle was the most difficult and discouraging—was to watch over my words. Very early on, He shared that I needed to stop declaring "I am sick" or "I have a fever" or "my liver is shutting down" or "my immune system isn't working properly." He told me never to come into agreement with the temporary circumstances and facts of the battle, but always to declare the eternal truth.

I did not lie about my condition. I did not ignore the reality of the symptoms that at times limited me. And I never denied that there were organs, glands and systems in my body that were being affected. But the Lord helped me understand the power of my words. He helped me see how to communicate the temporary facts honestly, while also standing on and declaring eternal truth. If I had to share with someone what was going on with me, I would say, "I'm currently overcoming a fever." Or I would say, "The doctors are working with me to strengthen my immune system."

Do you see the shift in language? Not "I am sick" or "I have a fever," but "I am overcoming." Not "my immune system isn't working well," but "my immune system is being strengthened." I was making positive decrees in the midst of negative situations, and the words commanded my body to overcome and be strengthened. They were also statements of faith that agreed with the eternal truth that no matter what was going on with my health in the moment, ultimately I was healed by the stripes of Jesus, and the full manifestation of that promise was on its way.

These words had impact. They had power. They strengthened my body and soul. The more I said them, the more I believed. The more I believed, the more I would say them. These words heartened me. They encouraged me. They reminded me of what my true portion was. They were in agreement with the promises of God, and they helped manifest those promises in my life. That is the power of our words.

Throughout the prolonged up-and-down journey with my health, the lesson of my words was one I had to be reminded of over and over again. Often, it seemed as if it were one step forward and two steps back. During those seeming setbacks, I would need to win the battle for my mind, will and emotions all over again. One of the ways I would do this was through the power of my words. I would make myself proclaim faith statements. Even when I did not feel like it, I would declare that I was healed by the stripes of Jesus and that the Holy Spirit was at work within me, quickening my mortal body (see Romans 8:11; 1 Peter 2:24). Just saying these things by faith, over and over and over again, would have an impact. Even if the symptoms in my body did not change in the moment, the state of my soul would. Declaring and thinking about how the very same Holy Spirit that raised Jesus from the dead was at work inside me would stir me. If the Holy Spirit was able to lift Jesus up out of the grave, then certainly He was able to lift me up out of the symptoms that were coming against me.

My words had impact. At first they heartened me, and then ultimately they helped bring forth increasing manifestations of the healing that was mine in Christ. In Mark 11:23, Jesus is mentoring the disciples about how to have radical impact in the earth on behalf of the Kingdom. During this lesson He mentions belief once, but three times He talks about the words we speak: "For assuredly, I say to you, whoever *says* to this mountain, 'Be removed and be cast into the sea,' and does not doubt in his heart, but *believes* that those things he *says* will be done, he will have whatever he *says*' (NKJV, emphasis added). Of course, belief is important. Faith is the very foundation of our salvation and our walk with God. But this lesson from Jesus makes it quite clear that the words we speak are also very important. They are a huge part of determining what occurs in our lives, and also what is released through our lives into the earth.

Speak Well of Yourself

One of the most important areas where we need to watch over our words is when we speak about ourselves. We cannot control what others say about us, but we can control what we say about ourselves.

The simplest way to watch over and steward the words you speak about yourself is to remember that you are made in God's image. You are made in the image of the Great I AM, so you should never make an "I am" statement about yourself that you would not make about Him.

You would not say, "The Great I AM is stupid."

You would never say, "The Great I AM is a loser."

You certainly would not say, "The Great I AM is sick and will never get better."

No! So do not ever declare over yourself, "*I am* stupid."

Do not say, "*I am* a loser."

Do not declare, "*I am* sick and will never get better."

Do not say anything about yourself that you know is not true about God. You are made in His image. Use your words to remind yourself of that every single day.

What do you think of the Great I AM? Do you think He is kind, loving, trustworthy, amazing, wonderful, powerful? Then those are the "I am" statements to speak over yourself: "*I am* kind." "*I am* loving." "*I am* amazing." "*I am* powerful."

You are not declaring that you are God. You are agreeing with His Word that you are wonderfully made in His image (see Genesis 1:26–28; Psalm 139:14). He is the Great I AM, and you are His very good creation. Let your words always agree with that truth.

Your Mouth Is the Gate

From the very beginning, God showed us the power of words and how we can use them to have an impact on reality. In Genesis 1 the earth was covered in darkness, and it was void and chaotic. God spoke "Let there be light" to shatter the darkness and establish Kingdom order. He spoke again (and again) to fill the earth with His divine creation. While we are by no means God, we are made in His image. We, too, can use our words to release light and bring forth the Kingdom. We can bless, encourage, exhort, edify, declare His truth and proclaim His Word. As we do that, darkness in our lives and darkness in the earth will be overcome, and circumstances that are difficult or confused will be brought into Kingdom order.

Do not be dismayed if you do not see a shift immediately when you speak powerful, positive words. Every time you choose to speak Kingdom truth, it has an impact. Keep winning the battle for your mind, will and emotions. Keep using the power of your words to fill your reality with life, light and love. You will see the victory.

We have talked quite a bit throughout these pages about how we are gates in the earth. I hope you are starting to understand what a powerful gate your mouth is. The average person speaks somewhere between ten thousand and fifteen thousand words a day. Even if you are at the low end of that, you are still releasing an amazing amount of "material" into your life every 24 hours. Will it be for good, or for ill? For life, or for death? For blessing, or for curses? You and only you can determine that, because you and only you have control over the power of your words.

BATTLE KEYS

Practical ways to apply the truths of this chapter in your life:

1. Have prophetic words or promises been spoken over your life that have yet to come to pass? Ask the Holy Spirit to help you remember if you have ever spoken words of doubt or negativity in regard to those promises—things like "I don't think it's ever going to happen," or "nothing good ever happens for me," or "I'll believe it when I see it." If so, repent of those negative words. Cover them with the blood of Jesus and command them to fall to the ground harmless and ineffective. Then replace them with confessions of faith, praise and thanksgiving, declaring that the Lord is trustworthy, His words are true and His promises always come to pass. Give thanks for any promises that *have* manifested in your life. If none come to mind right away, you can also give thanks for promises that came to pass in the Bible (like the coming of Messiah after hundreds of years of prophecy). Declare that the Lord is the same yesterday, today and forever, and that your long-awaited promise *will* come to pass, just like all those other promises of God.

2. Think of your favorite aspects about the character and nature of God. They could be that God is brilliant, that He is kind and that He never gives up. Now remember that you are made in His image, and your born-again

198

character and nature are in the very likeness of the character and nature of the Great I AM. Let this truth fill you afresh. As it does, begin to make "*I am*" decrees about yourself that line up with the supernatural reality that you are His "re-presentation" in the earth. For example:

- "*I am* . . . brilliant. I have the mind of Christ. All I have to do is ask my Father in heaven for wisdom, and He gives it to me in abundance. There is no situation, problem or challenge beyond my ability in Christ to deal with, solve and overcome. Because I am brilliant."

  (From 1 Corinthians 2:16; James 1:5; Daniel 1:17, 20; Philippians 4:13)

- "*I am* . . . kind. I show mercy and compassion to all whom I meet. I see the very best in everyone, and I always have an encouraging word to share with others. Because I am kind."

  (From 1 Corinthians 13:4; Matthew 9:36; John 1:47; 1 Corinthians 14:3)

- "*I am* . . . persistent. I never give up. I never give in. I never lose faith. Even if I experience a setback or failure, I know it is only temporary. I will learn from it. I will move forward. God turns everything to the good. In the end, I will triumph. Because I am persistent."

  (From 1 Corinthians 13:7, 8a; 2 Chronicles 15:7; Romans 8:28; James 1:12)

Declare your "*I am*" statements out loud every day for a week. Then at the beginning of a new week, think of three more aspects of God's character and nature that you admire and appreciate. Use these to create new "*I am*" statements to decree over yourself. Do this each week for three months. Hold on to all your "*I am*" decrees and use them over and over again. It is a simple and powerful way to use the gate of your mouth and the power of your words to bless yourself throughout the year.

3. Think of someone in your life who could use a boost. Ask the Lord for something positive, affirming and encouraging you could say to that person today. Call him or her and work the blessing into your conversation. If you do not happen to reach the person, leave a voicemail message speaking the blessing over him or her. After doing this with a few close friends, try expanding it. Ask the Lord for positive and affirming words for a family member, someone at work and for a person you encounter at random. See how many people you can use the power of your words to speak blessings to in a single day.

4. For one hour, commit to monitoring your language. Pay attention to the words you speak. If you catch yourself murmuring, complaining or saying something that is negative or full of fear and unbelief, ask the Holy Spirit to help you change your language so that you shift from a negative report to a positive one, from discouraging to encouraging, from cursing to blessing. For example, if you say something like, "I don't know if my son will ever stop running from God and embracing the ways of the world," you could change this to a positive declaration: "God is working on my son's heart. He is pursuing my boy with His truth and love. My son will know and serve the Lord one day."

8

Choosing to Live in Victory

These things I have spoken to you, so that in Me you may
have peace. In the world you have tribulation, but take courage; I have overcome the world.

John 16:33

In Christ you lack nothing. He has done all. He has won
all. And He has given all. Every victory. Every blessing.
Every promise. They are all already yours. I know it does
not always look and feel that way, but that is where the battle
comes in. The battle is not about laying hold of something
you do not have; it is about deciding whether or not you will
choose to agree with what is yours in Christ when it does not
look or feel that way. Will you choose to agree with God's
eternal truth in the midst of temporary circumstances, or
will you bow down to how things look and feel in the moment? This is the battle, and ultimately it will be won or lost
in your soul—the place of volition.

The enemy works overtime to highlight facts, situations and events to try to convince you that God will not come through, or that His promises are not for you. But it is a lie. Facts may be true in the moment. Situations may be real right now. Events may be something you need to deal with. But they are temporary. They are what the apostle Paul called "light and momentary afflictions" (see 2 Corinthians 4:17). Even though they rarely feel "light" or "momentary," compared to eternal truth that is what they are. Facts change. Situations shift. Events come and go. And the more you are willing to stand on and declare eternal truth in the midst of those facts, events and situations, the more quickly they will change, shift and go. That is the power of your faith.

The power of your soul is in choosing to stand strong in faith when nothing other than the Word of God and your born-again spirit says it makes any sense. That is the battle. The enemy's attacks, efforts and schemes are not the real issue. The real issue is how you respond to those attacks, efforts and schemes. The enemy is doing all he is doing to try to sucker you into using your authority to decide that you are defeated, busted and hopeless. He cannot make you be those things; he can only try to make you believe that you are those things. He wants to tempt you into using the power of your soul to choose to believe that God is not real or that His promises are not true. The enemy's lies, lures, tricks and traps are all aimed at convincing you to come into agreement with death, not life; curses, not blessings; defeat, not victory. He wants you to believe that the temporary balance of your checkbook declares that you will never have enough, instead of choosing to stand on the eternal truth that God will meet all your needs according to His riches in glory (see Philippians 4:19). He wants you to believe that the most recent medical report means that you will never be well, as opposed to choosing to stand on the eternal truth that you are healed by the stripes of Jesus (see Isaiah 53:5). The enemy wants you to believe that your prodigal's latest declaration of faithlessness is proof he or she will never come to know the Lord, as opposed to standing on the eternal truth that through your faith in Christ, all your household will be saved (see Acts 16:31).

There is power in choosing to live in victory. That is why the apostle Paul assured you, and every New Testament believer, that if you are willing to look beyond current problems and keep focused on the certainty of God's promises, you will see a greater glory break forth (see 2 Corinthians 4:17). This is what the enemy is afraid of. This is what the enemy is working against. He is terrified of your ability to bring heaven to earth through your decision to stay in faith in the face of challenges and difficulties.

Jesus did not mince words. He flat out said in John 16:33 that in this fallen world, there will be times when we face trials, troubles and tribulations. But in that same Scripture, He also reminded us that though we are in this world, we are also in Him. And in Him we can always know the peace of certain victory, because He has overcome the world. Not that He will overcome one day. But that He *has* overcome. That means anything that this fallen world can throw at us—and anything the enemy can throw at us in this fallen world—Jesus has already overcome. The word Jesus uses in this verse for *overcome* is *nikao* in the Greek, and it means "subdue, conquer, prevail, get the victory." He is being very clear: No matter what light and momentary affliction we are facing, no matter what fact, event or situation we are dealing with, it is done. He has won. It has been sorted, dealt with, subdued, conquered and overcome. He has prevailed. It is finished (see John 19:30; 1 John 3:8).

The victory is not in question. What is in question is whether or not we will choose to agree with and live in that victory. Jesus knows this is not always easy for us to do. He knows how hard the enemy works to stir us up and get us caught up in fear, doubt, despair and other negative thoughts and emotions. That is why He said for us to *take* courage. Or, as John 16:33 is translated in the King James Version, to "be of good cheer" even in the face of these challenges. You know what it is to take courage? You know what it is to choose to be of good cheer, even when good things are not happening? It is winning the battle for your mind, will and emotions. It is deciding to trust in Christ more than the report of your circumstances. It is choosing to live in victory because you know in Christ you already have it.

Choosing to live in victory is not denial of the light and momentary afflictions you are overcoming. It is not even pretending that the situations that do not feel light or seem momentary are not challenging. Choosing to live in victory is refusing to doubt eternal truth on the basis of temporary circumstances. Choosing to live in victory is stepping into your place of dominion stewardship in the earth and operating in Kingdom authority over the first, and most important, realm you are responsible for—yourself. It is realizing that the key to inhabiting the victory that Christ has given you is to take control of your soul, so that your mind, will and emotions don't get hijacked by fear, doubt, anger, self-pity and negativity.

Throughout Scripture, we see examples of what Jesus is helping the disciples understand in John 16:33. When the Lord is about to bring His people into a new level of authority, empowerment and manifestation of what He has given us, He begins by revealing the importance of our winning the battles of the soul realm and choosing to live in victory. Let's look at a few examples.

Be Strong and Courageous

In Joshua 1, the people of God were entering a new era and a new place. Everything was about to shift. The time of Moses was over. The people were on the brink of crossing into the Promised Land. They were about to come into the milk-and-honey, manifest blessings of God. The Lord was mantling a new leader for this new time—Joshua—the man He would use to bring the people into this new "realm." As the Lord was establishing Joshua in a new role, He did two things. First, He gave Joshua promises to stand on—words from the Lord that Joshua could be certain of, no matter what. He told Joshua, "Every place on which the sole of your foot treads, I *have given* it to you" (verse 3, emphasis added). The Lord also promised him that no enemy "will be able to stand before you *all the days of your life. . . . I will not fail you* or forsake you" (verse 5, emphasis added). In other words, God's promise to Joshua was that victory was certain—always!

The second thing the Lord did for Joshua was to give him instructions on how to inhabit this new "place" and move in this new authority. Those instructions included God telling Joshua three times to be "strong and courageous" (see verses 6, 7, 9), and not to "tremble or be dismayed" (verse 9). The other instruction the Lord gave Joshua was to be sure to obey His Word—to study it and meditate on it day and night. If Joshua did this, the Lord told him, he would prosper and succeed wherever he went, no matter what he faced (see verses 7–8).

Do you see it? God's instructions to Joshua—not to tremble or be dismayed, to be strong and courageous at all times, never to give in to fear or discouragement—were the Lord letting him know that the secret to operating in his new mantle of authority was to win the battle for his mind, will and emotions. God knew Joshua would face many battles and many enemies in the Promised Land. He also knew that victory was certain in every single one of them. After all, that was His promise to Joshua in verses 3 and 5. The only variable was whether or not Joshua, in his free will, would choose to believe and stand on those promises in the tough times. If he was willing to rise up as a dominion steward of himself and win the battles of the soul realm, then there was no battle he would not ultimately triumph in. All the days of his life he could live in the victory of the Lord—and lead others into it as well.

The key to all this was when the Lord instructed Joshua never to turn from His Word, to meditate on it day and night, and to be sure always to obey it. When God told this to Joshua, He was not setting him up with a quid-pro-quo set of religious requirements that would earn him the blessings and favor of God *if* he behaved. The Lord was reminding Joshua of the certainty of His Word and the power of holding His eternal truth above any temporary report, circumstance or situation.

The word for *obey* in verse 7—or, as our translation (the New American Standard Bible) and some others put it, "to do according to all the law"—is *shawmar* in the Hebrew. It has a very different meaning than what we think of when we hear the word *obey* in English. *Shawmar* is not about complying with a rigid set of rules, obligations, conditions or prerequisites in order to qualify for an agreed-upon reward if all terms are met. Rather, it means to "attend to, take heed, guard, protect, keep, wait for, preserve, [be] sure." The Lord was letting Joshua know that his key to living in victory was to *attend to* the Word of the Lord, *take heed* of it and *guard* his heart from ever doubting. God was letting Joshua know that no matter how things might look or feel in any given moment, if he was willing to *keep* his mind set on God's promises, allow them to *preserve* his faith and expectantly *wait for* them to manifest, then he could be *sure* of success—even in the midst of bad reports, difficult situations and attacks of the enemy.

Shawmar is basically the Hebrew word for winning the battle for your mind, will and emotions by choosing to live in the certain victory of the truth of God's Word. *Shawmar* is a reminder to focus on the eternal reality of "It is finished," even when it does not look or feel that way in the moment.

Joshua learned well the lesson of *shawmar*. We see a clear example of this in Joshua 6, when he approached the city of Jericho. This was the first major battle the Israelites faced after crossing into the Promised Land, and it looked to be a doozy. Jericho was the most fortified city in all of Canaan. Its walls were so massive that houses were built into them. It was ranged with warriors and weapons, and they were all ready and waiting for the Israelite army. Verse 1 puts it this way: "Now Jericho was tightly shut because of the sons of Israel."

As Joshua approached Jericho—the greatest stronghold in the land—it must have looked impenetrable. But the Lord spoke to Joshua and said, "I have given you Jericho, its king, and all its mighty warriors" (verse 2 NLT). Who could blame Joshua if his first thought was, *Really? It sure doesn't look as if You have given it to me. It looks as if they are armed to the teeth and ready to fight.* Joshua had a decision to make.

Was he going to believe the very real way things looked in the "now" of verse 1—that the stronghold of Jericho was tightly shut against him and the Israelites? Or was he going to trust in the word of the Lord in verse 2—that despite how things seemed, God had given him the city? Was he going to give greater weight to the very real, temporary circumstances that were staring him in the face, or to the eternal promises of God that wherever he went, no enemy could stand before him and he had the victory (see Joshua 1:3, 5)?

Joshua's "light and momentary affliction" was real; it was a massive fortified stronghold loaded with weapons and warriors. It was as real as that empty checkbook balance, bad medical report or belligerently wayward prodigal we talked about earlier. But for Joshua, none of it was as real as the word of the Lord. Joshua chose to trust in God and His promises. Joshua chose to *shawmar*.

Joshua chose to win the battle for his mind, will and emotions and not be swayed from eternal truth by the temporary facts. Joshua chose to live in victory, even when it did not look as though he was anywhere close to having it. And because of that, he eventually saw the victory manifest. It was a journey. It was a process. But he chose to walk through it all with the Lord day after day, trusting in His word above all else. And eventually, he saw a miraculous, "impossible" victory. The walls of Jericho tumbled down, and the Israelites took the city, destroying the enemy without losing a single man (see Joshua 6:3–27).

Why Are You Crying?

In John 20, everything was set up for the disciples to step into all the Lord had been sharing with them for the past three years. He had gone to the cross. He had defeated all of hell and death. And now, He was about to ascend to the right hand of the Father. But the disciples were wrestling with it all. Nothing had gone the way they were expecting. And each of them, in his own way, was struggling with the battle for his mind, will and emotions. Instead of choosing to live in victory, they were choosing to live in confusion, fear and doubt (see Matthew 26:31, 56; Mark 14:50).

After the crucifixion, Mary Magdalene was the first one to go to the tomb of the Lord (see John 20:1). When she got there, she discovered that the stone had been rolled away from the entrance and the body of Jesus was gone. She did not understand. She was overcome by emotion and began to weep (see verse 11). As she stood looking into the tomb, she saw two angels sitting where the body of Christ had been. They asked her, "Why are you crying?" (verse 13 NLT).

The angels were not being insensitive. They were not being cruel. The angels were aware that this was a difficult time for Mary (and for all the disciples), but they also knew that if she could not get control of her soul and win the battle for her mind, will and emotions, she would not be able to see past her limited understanding of the moment, to step into the monumental victory Jesus had won for her through the finished work of the cross.

Mary was caught up in what she saw as loss, and it was keeping her from being able to grab hold of heaven's perspective and see the great victory of the empty tomb. But she was not left on her own in this, and neither are you and I. Even in the very toughest times, when we are struggling the most with the battle for our mind, will and emotions, the Lord is with us. Mary glanced over her shoulder and noticed that someone was there with her. It was the Lord, but she did not recognize Him; she thought He was the gardener (see verses 14–15).

Grief, confusion, fear and self-pity can all blind us to God's ways—and even to His presence. Negative emotions can keep us from seeing divine opportunities when they are right in front of us. Which is why the unrecognized Risen Lord asked Mary the same question as the angels: "Why are you crying?" (verse 15 NLT).

He was not chastising her. He was not finding fault. He was not telling her to buck up and soldier on. He was helping her realize where she was emotionally, so she could move beyond that place and step into the victory that was available to her even though she did not yet see it. The Lord was coming alongside Mary in the battle for her mind, will and emotions.

Then Jesus went deeper. He went to the root of the issue. He asked her, "Whom are you looking for?" (see verse 15 NLT). He knew Mary was heartbroken because she was looking for the One she had known and loved and walked with. She was looking for what had been, as opposed to seeing what was now available to her. She was valuing the past, in peril of being so stuck in it that she could miss out on the glorious future the victorious Lord had for her. But in His great love for Mary, the Lord met her exactly where she was. He said her name. This brought her into the moment. It opened her eyes, and she proclaimed, "Teacher!" (see verse 16).

Mary was partway there. She now realized that this was not the gardener, but she still did not yet see Him for who He truly and fully was. She had called Him "Teacher" because she was still trying to relate to Him as what He had been when she had walked and talked with Him during His three-year ministry in the earth. Then the Lord lovingly told Mary to stop "clinging" to Him (verse 17). He was not saying, "Woman, give Me some space; you are suffocating Me!" The word for "clinging" that He used was *haptomai* in the Greek, and it means "to attach oneself to." The Lord was telling Mary not to attach herself merely to what He had been, but to see Him now for what He was, so that she could step into all He had accomplished and wanted to give her. To get there, she would need to get past the feelings she was wrestling with and be willing to think of the Lord in a new way. In other words, she would need to win the battle for her mind, will and emotions. If she did, she would step into a new realm, a new assignment and a new revelation of the restored relationship with the heavenly Father and all of His Kingdom that the victorious Lord had won for her (see verse 17).

Mary chose to live in victory. She chose to let go of grief, confusion, self-pity and doubt so that she could step out into this new era, new realm and new covenant. She did not cling to what had been, but embraced what now was. She went to the other disciples and let them know that she had seen the Risen Lord, and she began to spread His message (see verse 18).

As God does new things in our lives—as He answers the cry of our heart for "more!"—we may not always recognize or understand what is going on. We may not even always "see" Him in the circumstances that are the doorway into this new realm. But He is there (see Matthew 28:20), and He is helping us win the battle for our mind, will and emotions in the midst of all that is going on. During these times, it is key that we do not cling to what has been, or even what we have known of Him in the past. We can remember it. Cherish it. Draw strength from it. But we must not get so attached to it that we get stuck in what was, which will keep us from being able to move into what He has for us in the new season. All that He is and all that He has done are always ours. We never lose any of Him. But if we hold so tightly to one aspect or another of Him and His Kingdom that we are unwilling to embrace new aspects of relationship with Him, we might lose a chance to step into new revelation and new assignments. We might lose a chance to take new territories.

Focus on the Positive

We tend to think that it all would be so much easier if God would just straight out tell us what was going on. Yet that really is not the case. Being aware of God's plan does not save us from the battle for our mind, will and emotions. Not only because His ways can be so far beyond our natural understanding (see Isaiah 55:8–9), but also because we often miss the point, even when the Lord is very clear and direct with us.

Think of the disciples in Matthew 16:21–23. Jesus mapped it all out for them. He let them know step by step what was going to happen, right up to the point of His resurrection. He told them they were going to go to Jerusalem. Then He shared what would happen once they got there. He let them know that He would suffer many things at the hands of the elders, chief priests and scribes. He explained that He would be killed, but also that three days later, He would be raised from the dead.

How did the disciples respond? Did they say, "Thank You, Lord, for being so clear and direct with us. This is amazing! We really appreciate it. You've walked us through everything that will make it possible for the Kingdom to be reestablished in the earth, and for us to step into all that You have been telling us about for these past three years. This is so much easier to understand than all those parables"?

No! Peter actually goes off on Jesus and says, "God forbid it, Lord! This shall never happen to You!" (verse 22). Peter was so overwhelmed by what he perceived as a negative— Jesus being arrested, suffering and being killed—that he completely missed the amazing, mind-blowing, miraculous positive of Jesus being raised from the dead three days later.

Before you start judging Peter, realize that we do the same thing. The Lord is just as direct with us as He was with Peter and the disciples in Matthew 16:21. He has clearly mapped out for us in His Word what is in store for us. He will prosper us and bring us into a glorious future (see Jeremiah 29:11). He will always lead us in victory (see 2 Corinthians 2:14). He will rebuke the devourer (see Malachi 3:11). He will give us life in abundance (see John 10:10). He will heal all our diseases (see Psalm 103:3). He will meet all our needs according to His riches in glory (see Philippians 4:19). He will turn everything to the good (see Romans 8:28). And much, much more. Yet when we encounter tests, trials, difficulties and bad reports, just like Peter, we often allow those things to overwhelm us to the point of completely losing the plot in regard to the miraculous positives God has in store for us. In those moments, like Peter, we are caught up in fears, concerns and doubts. But as He was with Peter, the Lord is right there with us. If we are willing, He will help us get past our *self* and back into a Kingdom mindset, the same way He helped Peter (see Matthew 16:23–25).

Choosing to live in victory is choosing to focus on the Good News, even in the midst of challenging circumstances. It is not denying the challenges; it is choosing to focus on the positives, even in the midst of serious negatives. And there are always positives. Sometimes it takes real effort to shift our perspective enough to see them, but they are there.

I realize that statement is potentially offensive to those of you who are going through a great difficulty right now. Your flesh may want to rise up and say, *But you don't know what I'm dealing with, and how long I've been dealing with it!* And you are right. I don't. And while I absolutely do not want to make light of what you are going through, I do want to help you see victory in the face of it. The enemy wants you caught up in fear, self-pity, bitterness and offense. The enemy wants to lure you into making the same mistake that Peter did. He wants you to be so focused on the problems that you lose sight of the resurrection power of the Lord, which overcomes every manifestation of hell and death. The enemy wants you certain that there cannot possibly be any positives for you to focus on in the midst of the very real negatives you are dealing with.

Yes, it can take real effort to shift your focus from the negative to the positive, but you can do it because you can do all things through Christ who strengthens you. Start small. There is breath in your lungs. You have eyes to see the words on this page. You had the strength to open this book and hold your head up long enough to read this sentence. And then build from there. Is there food in your refrigerator? Do you have a good church? Is there one person you can call your friend? Have the Holy Spirit help you. Ask Him to bring things to mind that are positives you can focus on to remind you of the goodness of God in the midst of the negatives you are overcoming—things that will remind you that He is with you, and that He is leading you into a manifestation of the victory you are choosing to live in. The Lord loves you. He died for you. He saved you. There are so many positives for us to focus on just in the good news of the Gospel.

There Is Always Victory

I can relate to Peter. There were many times throughout the years of my battle to overcome chronic illness that the Lord had to help me break free of a wrong perspective or a negative focus. One of the most significant was a visitation I had just after returning home from four weeks of intensive in-patient treatment at an overseas clinic, where for eight to ten hours a day a highly regarded research physician and his team put me through a course of experimental drug and vitamin therapies. After all that time and all those treatments, I came home feeling sicker than ever, weaker than ever and more discouraged than ever. On top of it all, I also had a mountain of medical bills.

So there I was, sitting in my prayer chair, feeling lousy and feeling sorry for myself. I began to list off to the Lord how sad my situation was. I reminded Him of all I had been through—all the attacks of the enemy, all the bouts of sickness, all the symptoms, all the doctors I had seen, all the diagnoses I had received, all the treatments I had undergone, all the money I had spent, all the times I had rallied my faith, bolstered my hope, refocused in prayer—and for what? To be worse off than ever? It did not seem right. It did not seem fair. I was frustrated. I was angry. I felt . . . done. At one point, I even asked the Lord to either manifest my healing right now or take me home, because I could see no reason to continue this way.

He interrupted me with a question. He asked me to consider whether the greatest call upon my life—greater than my call to preach, greater than my call to the nations—was to stand in the midst of this extended battle and not budge from the truth that He is the Lord who heals. And whether that kind of unmoving faith could help launch a great healing revival that the next generation of ministers would walk in, all to His glory because He had found one He could trust with this battle, one who would not budge from believing and declaring that He is the Lord who heals, no matter what.

I sat for a moment, considering this. And then I asked Him a question: "Does that mean I won't ever see the manifestation of *my* healing?"

He immediately responded, *That is not what I said.*

He was firm, but also very tender. And somehow in that short response, He communicated volumes. It was like a veil of selfishness was lifted from my mind and my heart. All of a sudden, I realized what He was saying, what He was doing. It was crystal clear. He was helping shift my focus. He was helping me see that there is always good news. He was reminding me that even when—*especially* when—I could not see or sense Him working, He was still always there, always good and always bringing about something truly amazing.

He was helping me get my eyes off myself long enough to get past the negatives and remember that with God, there are always positives and always victory. In that moment, He helped me see that a big part of my wrestle was that I felt like a failure for the Kingdom, as if I had let the enemy take me out through sickness. I had gone from preaching and ministering at conferences and events around the world three or four times a month, to barely being able to do a Sunday service here and there on occasion. In that moment, He helped me see that part of my self-pity actually came from my being disappointed in myself because I had bought into a lie that my prayers "hadn't worked," that I had not won the battle even after all these years, and that I had become ineffectual for the Kingdom.

But in that moment, He helped me see that He was not disappointed in me, so I did not need to be disappointed in myself. He helped me see that I was not a failure. I was not ineffectual. I was not losing. I had not been taken out by the enemy. Just the opposite. By choosing to stand in faith again and again and again, I was actually having a great impact for the Kingdom. I was not a victim, but a victor. I was not on the sidelines, but actually in the very heat of the battle. In that moment, I knew I would see my healing fully manifest one day, but also that every moment of the journey had been worth it because every prayer had "worked," every prayer had had impact, every prayer had gone forth and accomplished what it was sent to do. Not only had I prayed powerful prayers, but my life itself had become a powerful prayer—not just for my healing, but for a wave of healings, a move of healings, a revival of healing that would one day break forth because again and again and again it had been declared in faith that Jesus is the Lord who heals!

After that encounter, I became even more fervent in prayer and intercession. Not just on behalf of myself, but on behalf of the Lord who heals, who has overcome every sickness and disease. On days when I had strength, I prayed. On days when I did not have very much strength, I still prayed. I knew that the power of my prayer and intercession was not in my physical strength, but in the eternal truth of God's Word. Sometimes I would get miracle testimonies from people I had prayed for, and I would rejoice that the manifestation of their healing had broken forth. But even if I never heard anything back, or even if it seemed as if nothing happened when I prayed, I still knew every prayer had effect, and that more momentum was building for the great wave of healing revival we will one day see.

I was more certain than ever that God was good, He was faithful and His Word was true. Period. It was not that I never had another challenging day, or a time when I had to win the battle for my mind, will and emotions all over again. I still have days like that at times, even now. It was that God had shown me that being in a battle did not make me a victim; it made me one of His triumphant warriors who had been entrusted with an assignment. He helped me realize that as a man of faith, living in victory is always just a choice away.

As Your Soul Prospers

In John 16, Jesus was making the disciples aware that everything was about to shift, everything was about to change. He wanted them to know that they were on the verge of stepping into all that He had been sharing with them for the past few years. Every promise. Every blessing. Everything. They were going to be mantled and empowered to operate in a remarkable expression of His complete authority, to bear witness of the reality of Him to the world around them.

It would be like nothing mankind had walked in since Adam and Eve were in the Garden, knowing the fullness of fellowship with God, and operating as His dominion stewards in the earth. But the Lord also knew that very little of it would come about in the way the disciples were thinking or expecting, so He assured them that even in the midst of challenges, they could be certain of the victory He was giving to them. He also let them know that the key to living in this victory was to *have* peace and to *take* courage. He told them, "These things I have spoken to you, so that in Me you may have peace. In the world you have tribulation, but take courage; I have overcome the world" (John 16:33). In other words, He was highlighting that the secret to walking in all He was giving to them was their winning the battle for their mind, will and emotions.

It is the same for you. Jesus has done all and won all. He has given you the victory. It is all just a decision away. As you have read through *Winning the Battle for Your Mind, Will and Emotions*, you have been enlightened, equipped and empowered. Grab hold of the truths the Holy Spirit has breathed upon in this book. Remember that you are a dominion steward in the earth, and that the first realm you are responsible for is yourself. Decide today that you will no longer let your circumstances affect the level of victory that you walk in, but instead that the level of victory you walk in will affect your circumstances.

The apostle John put it like this: "Prosper in all things and be in health, just as your soul prospers" (3 John 2 NKJV). The word for *prospers* that he used there is *euodoo* in the Greek, and one of its translations is "to succeed." What the apostle John is sharing with his friend Gaius, and with you, is what he learned from the Lord. You do not need to win victory over the enemy. You do not need to win victory to secure blessings. And you do not need to win victory to have favor with God. Jesus has done all that for you. You simply need to win victory over yourself. You need to succeed in the battle of the soul realm—the battle for your mind, will and emotions. When you do that, you will prosper in all things—because all things have already been given to you in Christ.

BATTLE KEYS

Practical ways to apply the truths of this chapter in your life:

1. Learn to *shawmar*. Think of a battle you are facing. Ask the Lord to give you a promise Scripture—a passage

from the Bible that you can study, meditate on, keep and take heed of. A verse that will help you guard your heart and preserve your faith. Use this Scripture to remind you again and again of the victory the Lord has given you in the situation that is before you. Commit to "walking" with God each and every day, as Joshua did around the city of Jericho—taking time to focus on the promise He has given you, mulling it over, knowing its truth. Do this each day, until the promise becomes a "shout" in you that is so loud, so sure and so certain that no "wall" of circumstances can keep you from entering into the manifest victory of His Word (see Joshua 6:1–21).

2. Practice positive thinking. Think of three positives in your life right now, no matter how small. Write them down. Take time each day to look at your list. Intentionally focus on those positives. Let them be reminders to you of the goodness and faithfulness of God in your life. Ask the Holy Spirit to bring more positives to your mind. As He does, add one or two things to your list each day. You can also make lists of positives that are specific to challenges you are in the midst of. For example, if you and your spouse are having a disagreement, do not let the temporary negatives of that situation so fill your mind, heart and focus that you lose sight of all the good things about your spouse. You married this person for a reason. You love this person. Get with God and ask Him to help bring to mind three things about your spouse that you love, like and enjoy. Write them down. Add to that list regularly. Anytime you hit a bump in your relationship, take the list out and focus on those positives until you are able to see how small and temporary the negatives are compared to all the amazing good in your spouse.

3. Learn to "die quietly." The place of "death" is one of the quickest routes to breakthrough and transformation in the Kingdom. Mary discovered this at the tomb of Jesus (see John 20:1, 11–18). The Lord helped Peter and the other disciples understand this when He taught them that the only way to truly gain Kingdom life was to be willing to give up their own lives for His sake (see Matthew 16:21–25). This is not a literal death, but a "dying" to self—a letting go of selfish agendas, personal ambition and the need to always understand. This can be one of our greatest battles—the self can be hard to "kill." But you can accelerate this process by being willing to silence the self and learn to "die quietly." What this means is quite literally to shut your mouth in the midst of the challenging times. Stop murmuring, stop complaining, stop telling everyone what a challenging time you are going through, stop rehashing over and over again all the details and difficulties, stop giving voice and life to how unfair and awful it all is. Jesus modeled how to do this. He was "like a sheep that is silent before its shearers" (Isaiah 53:7). For those of you who are like me—a verbal processor—this can be especially challenging. But it is very effective. Choosing not to give voice to the negative helps you stay focused on the positive. Choosing not to seek others for comfort and understanding stirs you to seek God for wisdom. "Death" comes before resurrection. Joshua led the Israelites around the city of Jericho for six days in absolute silence, and it made way for a supernatural victory. Learning to "die quietly" is a powerfully effective strategy that will help you quickly enter into victory in the battle for your mind, will and emotions.

Robert Hotchkin was splitting wood in the mountains of Montana in the autumn of 2002 when he was radically saved and forever changed by the first of many encounters with the love of Jesus. He went from being a mocker and persecutor of Christians to being a passionate lover of Christ. That passion for the Lord marks his ministry, and it is truly contagious.

Robert serves as one of the core leaders of Patricia King Ministries, is the apostolic leader of Men on the Frontlines and hosts the show *Heroes Arise*. He also travels the world, ministering with strong faith and releasing revelation, prophetic decrees, healings, miracles and the love of God. He is a carrier of the glory and a sparker of revival fires. People have been healed, refreshed, set free and empowered through his life. Robert's preaching, teaching and ministry inspire believers to grab hold of their restored relationship with the Father through the finished work of the cross and walk the earth as agents of impact for the Kingdom of God. His great desire is that every person, city, nation and region would know that God is good and that He really, really loves them!

Robert lives in Arizona with his wonderful wife, Yu-Ree. She loves the desert heat. He is still getting used to it.

Connect with Robert online and through social media so that he can continue to pour into you:

RobertHotchkin.com
MenontheFrontlines.com
Facebook: Official Robert Hotchkin
Twitter: @RobertHotchkin
Instagram: Robert Hotchkin
YouTube: Robert Hotchkin Channel
XPmedia.com: Robert Hotchkin Channel